ADAM AND EVE AFTER THE PILL

MARY EBERSTADT

ADAM AND EVE AFTER THE PILL

Paradoxes of the Sexual Revolution

IGNATIUS PRESS   SAN FRANCISCO

Cover photographs: © iStockPhoto.com

Cover design by John Herreid

© 2012 by Ignatius Press, San Francisco
All rights reserved
ISBN 978-1-58617-627-3
Library of Congress Control Number 2011940702
Printed in the United States of America ⊗

To my teachers past and present—
including Father William A. Ryan of Togo
and the late Norman Kretzmann,
professor of philosophy at Cornell

Contents

Acknowledgments

Thanks first and foremost to my friend Joseph Bottum, former editor of *First Things*. His confidence in allowing me to work out the argument *Adam and Eve after the Pill* in the pages of that magazine during the years of his editorship was the sine qua non of this book. Thanks also to the rest of the *First Things* team of those days, especially Mary Rose Somarriba, whose patience with the initial essays helped them to acquire a second life in these pages. *First Things* also graciously granted permission for these earlier versions of the chapters. These include, as originally titled, "The Will to Disbelieve" (first delivered as a speech to the Love and Fidelity Network in Princeton in December 2008), "What Does Woman Want?", "How Pedophilia Lost its Cool", "The Weight of Smut", and "The Vindication of *Humanae Vitae*".

The William E. Simon Foundation provided critical support for this book during the months that I completed the manuscript, and my gratitude goes out to them. Thanks also to the Lynde and Harry Bradley Foundation for their aid with this and other work in the year 2012.

Tod Lindberg, editor of *Policy Review*, is another longstanding friend who encouraged this book. He understands the intellectual fascination of what Friedrich Nietzsche called the "trans-valuation of values", i.e., the moral face of a world unbounded by the Judeo-Christian code. My interest in that subject led to earlier versions of two of these chapters: "Is Food the New Sex?" and "Is Pornography the New Tobacco?" Both were published in *Policy Review* in 2009 (issues 153 and 154, respectively), which grants permission for their use. Thanks also to John Raisian and Stephen Langlois of the Hoover Institution for their support of my research during the years these chapters were written.

Other friends and acquaintances subjected to this or that aspect of these pages via conversations and/or correspondence include Susan Arellano, David Blum, Gerard Bradley, Joe Carter, Catherine Chieco, Michael Duffy, Patrick Fagan, Andrew and Denise Ferguson, Robert George, Father Justin Huber, Liam Julian, Stanley Kurtz, Demetra Lambros, Mary Anne Layden, Tina Lindberg, Kathryn Jean Lopez, Ashley McGuire, Kara McKee, David Mills, Michael Novak and the late Karen Novak, Tina and P.J. O'Rourke, Father Arne Panula, Robert Royal, Austin and Cathy Ruse, Father Peter Ryan, Father William A. Ryan, Apoorva Shah, Luis Tellez, Gayle and Joel Trotter, George Weigel, and W. Bradford Wilcox, among the other people I can remember bothering here and there with the work of these pages.

Ignatius Press having become another happy home, I would also like to thank Father Joseph Fessio, Mark Brumley, Diane Eriksen, and the rest of the team for their confidence and care with the manuscript, as ever, and for their always helpful insights and clarifications.

As for the home that is literal as well as figurative, my gratitude goes out, also as ever, to Nicholas, Frederick, Catherine, Isabel, and Alexandra.

Introduction

Time magazine and Francis Fukuyama, Raquel Welch and a series of popes, some of the world's leading scientists, and many other unlikely allies all agree: No single event since Eve took the apple has been as consequential for relations between the sexes as the arrival of modern contraception.[1] Moreover, there is good reason for their agreement. By rendering fertile women infertile with nearly 100 percent accuracy, the Pill and related devices have transformed the lives and families of the great majority of people born after their invention. Modern contraception is not only a fact of our time; it may even be the central fact, in the sense that it is hard to think of any other whose demographic, social, behavioral, and personal fallout has been as profound.

For many decades now, prescient people have understood as much. Though these days contraception as such attracts

---

[1] Nancy Gibbs, "The 50th Anniversary of the Pill: So Small. So Powerful. And So Misunderstood", *Time* magazine cover story, May 3, 2010; Raquel Welch, "It's Sex O'Clock in America", CNN Opinion, May 7, 2010, http://articles.cnn.com/2010-05-07/opinion/welch.sex.pill_1_baby-s-father-attitude-proliferation?_s=PM:OPINION; Francis Fukuyama, *The Great Disruption: Human Nature and the Reconstitution of Social Order* (New York: Free Press, 1999), p. 64. See also the papal encyclicals *Casti Connubii* (1930) and *Humanae Vitae* (1968). As for scientists who agree on the Pill's unique importance, see Sharon Begley, "The Power of Big Ideas", about an online nomination by scientists of history's most critical inventions (*Newsweek*, January 4, 1998).

little interest in secular academia, being more or less simply
taken for granted as a fact of life, such neglect was not always
the rule. As early as 1929, for example, fabled social observer
Walter Lippmann was calling attention to the radical impli-
cations of reliable birth control—even explicitly agreeing with
the Catholic Church in his classic book *A Preface to Morals*
that modern contraception "is the most revolutionary practice in the history of sexual morals." [2] In 2010—the year
that the Pill celebrated its fiftieth anniversary—that early verdict appeared wholly vindicated, as an outpouring of reflections on that anniversary affirmed the ongoing and colossal
changes that optional and intentional sterility in women has
wrought. [3]

The technological revolution of modern contraception
has in turn fueled the equally widely noted "sexual
revolution"—defined here and elsewhere as the ongoing destigmatization of all varieties of nonmarital sexual activity,
accompanied by a sharp rise in such sexual activity, in diverse
societies around the world (most notably, in the most
advanced). And though professional nitpickers can and do
quibble about the exact nature of the connection between
the two epochal events, the overall cause and effect is plain
enough. It may be possible to imagine the Pill being invented
without the sexual revolution that followed, but imagining
the sexual revolution without the Pill and other modern
contraceptives simply cannot be done.

Like the technological revolution that occasioned it,
this sexual revolution, too, has long attracted the attention
of social observers. In 1956, for example, the towering

[2] Walter Lippmann, *A Preface to Morals* (New York: MacMillan, 1929), p. 291.
[3] Perhaps the most thorough example in the popular press was *Time* magazine's cover story by Gibbs, "50th Anniversary of the Pill".

twentieth-century sociologist Pitirim Sorokin—founder of Harvard's Department of Sociology—published a short book called *The American Sex Revolution*.[4] Written for a general audience and much discussed in its time, it forcefully linked what Sorokin variously called "sex freedom" and "sex anarchy" to a long list of what he argued were critical social ills, including rising rates of divorce and illegitimacy, abandoned and neglected children, a coarsening of the arts high and low, and much more, including the apparent increase in mental disorders. "Sex obsession", argued Sorokin, now "bombards us continuously, from cradle to grave, from all points of our living space, at almost every step of our activity, feeling, and thinking."[5]

Around the same time, another celebrated secular Harvard sociologist, Carle Zimmerman, published his masterwork of history and sociology called *Family and Civilization*.[6] Though less immediately concerned with the sexual revolution as such than Sorokin had been in his more popularized text, Zimmerman's work likewise casts obvious, albeit tacit, criticism upon the social changes unleashed by modern contraception. *Family and Civilization* repeatedly linked declines in civilization to the features of what the author called "the atomistic family" type, including rising divorce rates, increasing promiscuity, juvenile delinquency, and neglect of children and other family responsibilities. These were features of modern society that Zimmerman, like Sorokin

---

[4] Pitirim Sorokin, *The American Sex Revolution* (Boston Mass.: Porter Sargent, 1956); see, particularly, chapter 2.

[5] Ibid., p. 54.

[6] Carle C. Zimmerman, *Family and Civilization* (New York: Henry Holt, 1947). See also the reprinted edition, edited by James Kurth (Wilmington, Del.: ISI Books, 2008). Subsequent citations refer to the ISI Books edition.

(and many other people in those days), judged to be self-evidently malignant. "The United States", Zimmerman concluded, "will reach the final phases of a great family crisis between now [1947] and the last of this century"—one "identical in nature to the two previous crises in Greece and Rome".[7]

Of course one need not be a Harvard sociologist to grasp that the technological severing of nature from nurture has changed some of the most elemental connections among human beings. Yet plainly, the atmosphere surrounding discussion of these changes has changed radically between our own time and that of the mid-twentieth century. What Zimmerman felt free to say in the 1940s and Sorokin in the 1950s about the downside of changing mores are by and large not things that most people feel free to say about our changed moral code today—not unless they strive to be written off as religious zealots or as the blogosphere's laughingstock du jour.

Again, as the celebrations of the Pill's fiftieth anniversary went to show, the sexual revolution is now not only a fait accompli for the vast majority of modern men and women; it is also one that many people openly embrace. Fifty years after the Pill's approval and counting, it is beyond question that liberationists and not traditionalists have written the revolution's public legacy across the West.

In this standard celebratory rendition, the sexual revolution has been a nearly unmitigated boon for all humanity. Along with its permanent backup plan, abortion, it has liberated women from the slavery of their fertility, thus freeing them for personal and professional opportunities they could not have enjoyed before. It has liberated men, too, from their former chains, many would argue—chiefly from

[7] Ibid., p. 274.

the bondage of having to take responsibility for the women they had sex with and/or for the children that resulted. It has also enriched children, some would posit, by making it easier to limit family size, and hence share the pie of family wealth and attention among fewer claimants. "In my mind," as one modern historian summarized the standard script, "there can be no doubt that, on the whole, the sexual revolution of the '60s and '70s improved the quality of life for most Americans."[8]

It is the contention of this book that such benign renditions of the story of the sexual revolution are wrong. That is to say, they are critically incomplete when measured against the weight of the evidence now before us.

Thus the chapters ahead tell a different version of what the sexual revolution has wrought than the Panglossian version that is standard today. They examine from different angles a wide body of empirical and literary and other evidence about what really happened once nurture was divorced from nature as never before in history. My aim in these pages is to understand in a new way certain of the human fallout of our post-Pill world—to shed light on what Sorokin once provocatively and probably correctly called a revolution "more far-reaching than those of almost all other revolutions, except perhaps the total revolutions such as the Russian".[9]

The evidence presented in the following chapters, I believe, roundly confirms two propositions that are—or ought to be—deeply troubling to serious people. First, and contrary to conventional depiction, the sexual revolution has proved

[8] David Allyn, *Make Love, Not War: The Sexual Revolution: An Unfettered History* (New York: Little, Brown, 2000; repr., New York: Routledge, 2001), preface to the Routledge edition, p. ix.

[9] Sorokin, *American Sex Revolution*, p. 14.

a disaster for many men and women; and second, its weight has fallen heaviest on the smallest and weakest shoulders in society—even as it has given extra strength to those already strongest and most predatory. For decades now, and apparently out of view of many people telling the tale, a compelling record has been building of the real costs that have been mounting since procreation became so effectively amputated from sexual behavior for so many people. It is a record rich now in detail from a variety of sources ranging from the social sciences—especially psychology and sociology—to more microscopic accounts of the revolution's real and permanent consequences in many lives. Like a mosaic, it is also a record that reveals and sheds light variously depending on which angle we choose to view.

Revealing that mosaic is the substance of this book. Chapter 1 concerns the contemporary secular intellectual backdrop inherited from the tumultuous 1960s. For decades now, it argues, the negative empirical fallout from the sexual revolution, while plain to see, has persistently been met with deep and entrenched denial among academic and other cultural authorities. So thoroughgoing is this denial, the chapter details, that it bears comparison to the deep denial among Western intellectuals that was characteristic of the last great debate that ran for decades—namely, the Cold War. Hence, the subtitle is "The Will to Disbelieve", which takes its name from a famous essay on intellectual denial from that other debate past. This opening of the book examines the evidence of such intellectual denial and the probable reasons for it.

The book then moves from theory to the ground, as it were, to examine the effects of the sexual revolution on actual human beings: women, children, and men. "What Is the Sexual Revolution Doing to Women? *What Does Woman*

Want?", a chapter examining trends in current fashionable writing about women and marriage, exhumes the pervasive themes of anger and loss that underlie much of today's writing on romance. This chapter includes discussion of the latest sociological literature arguing for the "paradox of declining female happiness"—that is, the unexplained gap between the unprecedented freedoms enjoyed by today's women and their simultaneous increasing unhappiness as measured by social science. The fact that women disproportionately bear the burdens of the sexual revolution, I argue here, might explain that hitherto unexplained paradox.

The following chapter, "What Is the Sexual Revolution Doing to Men? *Peter Pan and the Weight of Smut*", examines more paradoxical fallout from the revolution. Even as widely available contraception and abortion have liberated men from husbandhood and fatherhood, it has also encouraged in many a new and problematic phase of prolonged adolescence—what sociologist Kay S. Hymowitz has perspicaciously identified as "pre-adulthood".[10] Then there is the other paradoxical consequence of sexual liberation: widespread pornography on a scale and with a verisimilitude never seen before. This chapter cites interesting and recent work by psychologists, psychiatrists, sociologists, and other experts on a range of issues relating to Internet pornography: the sharp rise in pornographic addiction, the evidence of serious psychological problems of the addicted, the chilling effect of increasing pornography in the public square, and other measures of social harm.

Chapter 4, "What Is the Sexual Revolution Doing to Children? *The 'Pedophilia Chic', Then and Now*", covers one uniquely

---

[10] Kay S. Hymowitz, *Manning Up: How the Rise of Women Has Turned Men into Boys* (New York: Basic Books, 2011).

disturbing legacy of sexual liberation, which is the assault unleashed from the 1960s onward on the taboo against sexual seduction or exploitation of the young. This chapter argues that ironically, the Catholic priest-boy sex scandals that erupted in 2002—which evoked widespread revulsion across the West at these repeated violations of the taboo against sex with the young—have effectively served to interrupt this profoundly destructive former trend. Interestingly, this makes the taboo against sex with youngsters the only one of those considered in this book in which some "rollback" of the sexual revolution has been demonstrated.

Chapter 5, "What Is the Sexual Revolution Doing to Young Adults? *What to Do about Toxic U?*", examines in detail what may be ground zero of the sexual revolution today: the secular American campus. Using sources ranging from social science to popular culture, it sifts the ingredients of the toxic collegiate social brew made possible by the sexual revolution. The feral rates of date rapes, hookups, and binge drinking now documented on many campuses, this chapter argues, are direct descendants of the sexual revolution—one whose central promise is that women can and should be sexually available in the name of liberation, which translated into the reality of the modern campus has empowered and largely exonerated predatory men as never before.

Chapters 6 and 7 move back from the ground to a more abstract plane to examine other society-wide changes wrought by the revolution—in particular, its effect on social mores. They focus on what Friedrich Nietzsche called "the trans-valuation of values", meaning the ways in which the existing moral code would become transformed in a social order no longer centered on Judeo-Christianity. Such a transvaluation, I argue, is being wrought by the revolution in ways we are only beginning to understand. Chapter

6, subtitled "Is Food the New Sex?", argues that the morality once attached to sexual behavior has been transferred onto an unlikely yet fascinating substitute—matters of food. Chapter 7, subtitled "Is Pornography the New Tobacco?", similarly traces the stunning parallels between yesteryear's laissez-faire attitudes about one widely accepted substance—tobacco—and today's laissez-faire attitudes about the substance of pornography.

The book's closing chapter examines what may be the ultimate of the many paradoxes ushered in by the collision between the sexual revolution and human nature itself. "The Vindication of *Humanae Vitae*" examines the remarkable predictions made in that watershed document just a few years after the Pill itself appeared and examines a large historical irony: that one of the most reviled documents of modern times, the Catholic Church's reiteration of traditional Christian moral teaching, would also turn out to be the most prophetic in its understanding of the nature of the changes that the revolution would ring in. This chapter explores the extraordinary irony of our own particular moment in time, half a century after the sexual revolution—one in which every prediction made by Paul VI has been vindicated, even as the traditional Christian teaching against artificial contraception has come to be reviled by its adversaries and abandoned by Christians themselves as never before.

One final note: These chapters are indeed, as the title suggests, reflections—not manifestos or screeds or roadmaps to activism. It is my hope that readers will bring to them the same spirit with which the pages ahead were written: that of seeking sincerely and without cant to understand something of the manifold and unprecedented fallout of what may yet turn out to be the most consequential social revolution of all.

1 The Intellectual Backdrop

The Will to Disbelieve

Imagine for a moment that much of the world is living under a set of ideas that has manifestly awful economic, social, and moral consequences. Imagine, in fact, that one of the most obvious things *about* the world is the negative impact of those ideas on the people who live under them—which is why some scholars have toiled long and hard to assemble an empirical record of the influence of these ideas, showing the various ways in which they are bad for human beings.

Now imagine one more step. Imagine that, despite the empirical evidence about the human costs of those pernicious ideas, many people, including many or even most leading scholars, ignore those problematic facts. Some simply deny the data. Others try to explain them away as artifacts of something—anything—other than the bad ideas in question. Still other people, perhaps most perverse of all, argue that the consequences of these ideas are actually *good*—as in, they might *seem* bad to particularly unenlightened souls, but they make perfect sense once one's consciousness is elevated in the right direction.

If it seems incredible that otherwise reasonable, educated people in possession of damning empirical evidence would want to ignore it rather than change their minds, rest assured that it isn't. In fact, this picture of intellectual denial captures perfectly what went on for decades among educated people in the advanced West, over a not inconsequential matter that was resolved around the time when many of today's college students were born.

The matter was, of course, the Cold War. Incredible as it seems in retrospect, even to those who witnessed some of those years, the moral facts of the Cold War remained disputed at the highest intellectual levels, especially on American campuses, until about two seconds before the Berlin Wall came down. Yes, incredibly enough—and despite the fact that most other people on earth knew exactly what to think about communism, especially those unfortunate enough to live under it—there was no intellectual unanimity in the West during the decades leading up to 1989 about whether communist ideas and governments, in practice, had proved to be a human disaster.

In fact, to the extent that elite opinion on the subject did exist, it lined up in the majority quite the other way. In universities above all, especially elite universities, government and political science departments were dominated by strains of what was known as anti-anticommunism—in other words, by the idea that being against communism was somehow worse than being in favor of communism.

Astonishing as it seems today, some professors and intellectuals throughout the Western struggle against communism were outright Marxists. Others took a more nuanced view. They argued that, whatever the communists were doing, the capitalists and governments of the West were just as bad—or perhaps even worse. This line of argument was dubbed by (and deplored by) anticommunist critics as "moral equivalence". Of course, the most interesting thing here is the word "equivalence"—which at least implies that the communists were as bad as we were. In truth, though, many other critics of Western capitalism did not think the systems morally equivalent at all. They thought it obvious that communism was superior.

Still other scholars and intellectuals who stood against supposedly simple-minded anticommunism took a different tack. They argued that the Cold War was a "false construct", meaning that the differences between communism and capitalism were more superficial than they appeared. One subset of this line of reasoning was something called "convergence theory", according to which the United States and the Soviet Union—despite appearances—were actually behaving more like each other all the time.

I once took a rather sophisticated college class from one of the extremely convinced professorial leaders of this wing of thought, in 1979—a year in which, just for instance, forty thousand soldiers and officers of the Soviet communists marched into Afghanistan at Christmastime and proceeded to wage a war against civilians that stands distinguished in its wanton ferocity toward innocents even today. Yet even events like these did not upend the ideas of sophisticates intent on ignoring the evidence of the time and obeying the unwritten imperative to put the United States in the wrong. If one had asked most intellectuals and professors of the time whether the Cold War was morally clear-cut, and whether or not communism was causing misery on an unprecedented scale, one would have witnessed some combination of the responses just described—rounding the bases of denial, heated denial, and damned denial.

In retrospect, this formidable perversity—this otherwise inexplicable act of intellectual abdication—was more than just an outbreak of intellectual slumming. It was, in fact, one of the defining features of the Cold War. The denial stretched across the Western intelligentsia from Seoul to Boston, Oslo to Buenos Aires, and just about every point in between, wherever people clever enough to ignore the evidence could invent seemingly sophisticated reasons for doing so. Such profound and systematic resistance to the empirical facts was dubbed by the stalwart anticommunist Jeane Kirkpatrick as the "will to disbelieve", in an essay by that same name—a fine phrase that deserves resurrecting in the context of this book, for reasons that will be explained.

I have dwelt on this analogy to the Cold War because it illuminates a related problem that so often seems inexplicable in our own time: the powerful will to disbelieve in the harmful effects of another world-changing social and moral force. That would be the sexual revolution, or the destigmatization and demystification of nonmarital sex and the reduction of sexual relations in general to a kind of hygienic recreation in which anything goes so long as those involved are consenting adults. Such a world is one that liberationist philosophers have dreamed of for centuries now, and, as most people who are now adults could quickly testify, such a world is indeed ours today. About that much concerning the legacy of the sexual revolution, there is little doubt anywhere.

What is not widely agreed on, however, is the nature of the *fallout* from the revolution. Such a lack of consensus is interesting, because the empirical record by now weighs overwhelmingly against the liberationists—again, quite similarly to the way in which the moral record of communism weighed against the communists, even as many intellectuals in the West continued to deny it.

To say as much is not to say that the sexual revolution has caused anything like the Gulag archipelago or some of the other more dramatic legacies of communism (which apologists for Marxism and Marxist regimes used to call "excesses"). It is not to say that the sexual revolution is the root of all evil, any more than any other single momentous historical development is the root of all evil. It is to say, however, that the similarities between today's intellectual denials of the costs of the sexual revolution and yesterday's intellectual denials of the costs of communism are striking— and for those who are *not* in denial about what's happening, the similarities between these two phases of intellectual history line up uncannily well.

Consider just a few of the likenesses between these two epochal events in modern intellectual history. In both cases, an empirical record has been assembled that is beyond refutation and that testifies to the unhappy economic, social, and moral consequences. Yet in both cases, the minority of scholars who have amassed the empirical record and drawn attention to it have been rewarded, for the most part, with a spectrum of reaction ranging from indifference to ridicule to wrath.

The empirical record today on sex documents the overall benefits of marriage and monogamy, beginning with the married partners themselves. As numerous social scientists have shown, for example, monogamous married people score better on all kinds of measures of well-being.[1] A wealth of other data testifies to the proposition that families headed by a married couple—including disadvantaged families—are better off than those headed by a cohabiting couple.[2]

[1] See, for example, Linda J. Waite and Maggie Gallagher, *The Case for Marriage: Why Married People Are Happier, Healthier, and Better Off Financially* (New York: Doubleday, 2000; repr., New York: Broadway Books, 2001). See also Claire M. Kamp Dush and Paul R. Amato, "Consequences of Relationship Status and Quality for Subjective Well-Being", *Journal of Social and Personal Relationships* 22 (October 2005): 607–27.

[2] See, for example, Robert I. Lerman, "Impacts of Marital Status and Parental Presence on the Material Hardship of Families with Children", and "How Do Marriage, Cohabitation, and Single Parenthood Affect the Material

Then there is the small library now known under the rubric of "happiness studies". Women whose husbands are the breadwinners tend to be happier than other women.[3] Men who are married earn more and work harder than men who are single.[4] Conversely, promiscuity among teenagers and young adults appears closely related to educational failure and other problems such as alcohol and drug abuse.[5] Numerous authors have also shown that widespread divorce and unwed motherhood—two more offspring of the sexual revolution—are not only detrimental for many individuals but also costly for society.[6]

Sara McLanahan is another researcher who has painstakingly added to the store of knowledge about the downside of the sexual revolution—beginning with the days when she seemed a lone voice in a liberationist wilderness. Her seminal 1994 book, *Growing Up with a Single Parent*, coauthored with Gary Sandefur, features on its first page one of the most succinct indictments of the sexual revolution yet written:

> We have been studying this question for ten years, and in our opinion the evidence is quite clear: Children who grow up with only one biological parent are worse off, on average,

---

Hardships of Families with Children?", both published by the U.S. Department of Health and Human Services, 2002.

[3] See W. Bradford Wilcox and Steven L. Nock, "What's Love Got to Do with It? Equality, Equity, Commitment, and Women's Marital Quality", *Social Forces* 84, no. 3 (March 2006), pp. 1321–45.

[4] H. Chun and I. Lee, "Why Do Married Men Earn More: Productivity or Marriage Selection?", *Economic Inquiry* 39, no. 2 (April 2001): 307–19.

[5] See, for example, Henry J. Kaiser Family Foundation, "Substance Use and Sexual Health among Teens and Young Adults in the U.S.", Fact Sheet, February 2002.

[6] See, for example, Jessica Gavora, "Single Women as a Threat to Freedom", in Adam Bellow, ed., *New Threats to Freedom* (Conshohocken, Pa.: Templeton Press, 2010), pp. 56–66.

than children who grow up in a household with both of their biological parents, regardless of the parents' race or educational background, regardless of whether the parents are married when the children are born, and regardless of whether the resident parent remarries.[7]

In the years since, those words and formulations like them have been fighting words among sociologists—with the majority lining up, sometimes ferociously, opposite McLanahan and like-minded thinkers. It's not that these scholars are unaware of the evidence; it's rather that they feel forced to explain it away. Such is the deep desire to disbelieve that shapes—and misshapes—so much of what we read about sex today.

Or consider more recent evidence of the revolution's toll. One is an interesting book published in 2005 by Elizabeth Marquardt entitled *Between Two Worlds: The Inner Lives of Children of Divorce*.[8] Based on a 125-question survey administered with her co-researcher Norval Glenn to two groups—those who had grown up in divorced homes on the one hand, and those from intact homes on the other—Marquardt's results show clearly the higher risks of dysfunction and disturbance that follow many of the former into adulthood.

Just how different is the difference that Marquardt and Glenn turn up between their samples? Begin with a few practicalities—say, whether the family operates as a center of gravity or not. For example, 32 percent of children of divorce say their family was not in the habit of sharing a daily meal—compared to 8 percent of the children of intact

---

[7] Sara McLanahan and Gary Sandefur, *Growing Up with a Single Parent: What Hurts, What Helps* (Cambridge, Mass.: Harvard University Press, 1994).

[8] Elizabeth Marquardt, *Between Two Worlds: The Inner Lives of Children of Divorce* (New York: Crown Books, 2005).

homes.[9] Almost two-thirds of the divorced sample reports that "it was stressful in my family",[10] compared to 25 percent of the intact sample. Only one-third of the divorced sample can strongly agree with the statement "children were at the center of my family"[11]—as opposed to 63 percent of the intact sample. Many more examples confirm the perhaps unsurprising point: Broken homes have less time and room for kids than those that are intact.

Then there are the more nebulous but nevertheless striking differences in outlook. Judith Wallerstein had perspicaciously cited as common among her subjects "the fear that disaster was always waiting to strike without warning".[12] This apprehensiveness is also confirmed by the subjects in *Between Two Worlds*. Numerous of Marquardt's subjects—like the author herself—report a generalized apprehensiveness and dread of the world lasting well into adulthood. As one puts it and is echoed by others, "I always felt like I was watching out for something to go wrong. Not that I thought I was going to die or anything like that. But I always felt like things were lurking around corners."[13]

Marquardt's work among that of many others brings us to the moral core of the sexual revolution: the abundant evidence that its fruits have been rottenest for women and children. Even people who pride themselves on politically correct compassion, who criticize conservatives and religious believers for their supposed lack of feeling, fail to see the contradiction

[9] Ibid., p. 87.
[10] Ibid., p. 54.
[11] Ibid., p. 38.
[12] Judith Wallerstein, Julia M. Lewis, and Sandra Blakeslee, *The Unexpected Legacy of Divorce: The 25 Year Landmark Study* (New York: Hyperion, 2001), p. xxxiv.
[13] Marquardt, *Between Two Worlds*, p. 64.

between their public professions of compassion in other matters and their private adherence to a liberationist ethic.

This resolute refusal to recognize that the revolution falls
heaviest on the youngest and most vulnerable shoulders—
beginning with the fetus and proceeding up through children and adolescents—is perhaps the most vivid example of
the denial surrounding the fallout of the sexual revolution.
In no other realm of human life do ordinary Americans
seem so indifferent to the particular suffering of the smallest and weakest. Our campuses especially ring with the self-
righteous chants of those protesting genocide in Darfur, or
wanton cruelty to animals, or gross human rights violations
by oppressive governments such as China's. These are all
real problems about which real students shed real tears. Such
selective deployment of compassion is one of the more curious features of our time. People who in any other context
would pride themselves on defending the underdog forget
just who that underdog is when the subject is the sexual
revolution.

Yet as many people honestly did *not* realize when all this
started, the sexual revolution—specifically, the part of it that
marches under the slogan that a family is whatever someone says it is—has specifically and especially blighted the
lives of many, many children. Boys and girls without fathers
in the home, as generations of studies and social scientists
have shown by now, suffer emotional, financial, educational,
and other problems at higher rates than their peers.[14] They
are at higher risk for a variety of behavioral and mental

---

[14] Boys of never-married mothers, to take just one example that has been
repeatedly documented, are more likely to be suspended from school, to fail
in school, and to exhibit behavioral disorders. See, for instance, James Q.
Wilson, "In Loco Parentis: Helping Children When Families Fail Them",
The Brookings Review, Fall 1993, pp. 12–15.

disorders.[15] They are more likely to go to prison. As another pioneering writer, David Blankenhorn, took a whole book to explain—perfectly titled *Fatherless America*—not having a father in the home can predict all kinds of unfortunate results. Just for one, children whose mothers are divorced or unmarried are far more likely to suffer physical abuse in the home than are children with biological parents.[16]

That kind of empirical evidence abounds for those who need it; for those who do not, mere testimony of those afflicted might do. And evidence abounds, as well, quite apart from the social science. Contemporary rock and rap, for instance, are driven in significant measure by the fallout from the sexual revolution; their predominant themes (apart from sex itself) include broken homes, broken families, mom's abusive boyfriends, sexual predators, and the rest of the revolution's effects.[17]

And just as so many passionate and enlightened people ignore the fact that society's younger and weaker members have been damaged disproportionately by a Zeitgeist that favors the older and stronger, so too do they ignore this

[15] Teenagers from broken homes are both more likely to commit suicide and more likely to suffer from psychological disorders than teenagers with both biological parents at home. See, for example, David A. Brent et al., "Post-Traumatic Stress Disorder in Peers of Adolescent Suicide Victims: Predisposing Factors and Phenomenology", *Journal of the American Academy of Child and Adolescent Psychiatry* 34 (1995): 19.

[16] David Blankenhorn, *Fatherless America: Confronting Our Most Urgent Social Problem* (New York: Basic Books, 1995). On the disparities between families headed by married couples and those by single parents, see also Kay S. Hymowitz, *Marriage and Caste in America: Separate and Unequal Families in a Post-Marital Age* (Lanham, Md.: Ivan R. Dee, 2006).

[17] For an analysis of the centrality of the theme of family breakup in contemporary rock and rap, see Mary Eberstadt, "Eminem is Right", *Policy Review*, no. 128 (December 2004/January 2005): pp. 19–32.

related fact: The sexual revolution has also been a disaster for many women. Yet like hostages in the grip of Stockholm syndrome, feminists—above almost all other interest groups, with the possible exception of pornographers—cling to the defense of the sexual revolution. How many feminist-minded students who demonstrate for abortion rights realize that in many parts of the world, including the United States, girls are more likely to be aborted than boys?

Likewise, most American campuses have made it their business these days to train women against potential rapists. One recent such program at Princeton comes with a nifty online video, showing women being trained to yell and crouch and kick in strategically obvious places. No one would protest women defending themselves. But seeing just how omnipresent these kinds of classes and workshops are on campus, can't we wonder: Would we really need them so much if our campuses were a little less libertine, and the line between a plastered date and a real live rapist were a little easier to draw in the first place?

Though it's regarded as outrageous to say so in our metrosexual times, women remain far more vulnerable than men to physical abuse. Women who are divorced or unmarried are far more likely—twice as likely, according to one study—to suffer physical abuse than are women in an intact marriage.[18] To emphasize the ways in which sexual liberationism has injured women is not to say that men are unaffected. But with many men, the sexual revolution seems more like a slow-acting virus whose damage does not become apparent till much later in life. As Maggie Gallagher and

[18] See Gallagher and Waite, *The Case for Marriage*. See especially chapter 11, "Is Marriage a Hitting License?", pp. 150–60, which summarizes numerous studies to show that domestic violence is more likely outside of marriage than within it.

Linda Waite, among other researchers, have emphasized, divorced men have higher rates of depression, alcoholism, and other forms of "risk taking"—including such pedestrian oversights as failing to go to the doctor.[19]

For women, though, the fallout from the revolution appears more immediate and acute. It is women who have abortions and get depressed about them, women who are usually left to raise children alone when a man leaves for someone else, women who typically take the biggest financial hit in divorce, and women who fill the pages of such magazines as *Cosmopolitan* and *Mirabella* and chatty websites like *Salon* with sexual doublespeak. Just look at any one of those sources—or any random segment of women's morning talk shows or other popular "chick" fare like the television series *Sex and the City*. All reveal a wildly contradictory mix of chatter about how wonderful it is that women are now all liberated for sexual fun—and how mysteriously impossible it has become to find a good, steady, committed boyfriend at the same time.

It's as if, say, People for the Ethical Treatment of Animals were to put out magazines that were half pitches for vegetarianism and half glossy pages of pork and beef and chicken simmering in sumptuous sauces. If something like *that* were to happen, people would notice the contradiction. But because of the will to disbelieve in some of the consequences of the sexual revolution, they don't when the subject is sex.

If the will to disbelieve was powerful in the West during the Cold War years quite despite the easily available facts about communism, just imagine how much more powerful is the will to disbelieve in the facts about the sexual revolution. As Malcolm Muggeridge once observed, "People

---

[19] See ibid., especially chapters 4 through 9.

do not believe lies because they have to but because they want to." And it's hard to imagine wanting to believe anything more than the notion that one can enjoy sex on any terms without penalty. That's part of what the empirical facts are up against here—nothing less than human nature.

So how do those in the intellectual minority who are in possession of the facts, who are not in denial about them, break through this profound resistance? One guideline might be, the same way renegade thinkers did during the Cold War—by never giving up on patiently discussing the actual record of the world as it is, no matter how resolutely the other side ignores or disdains you. At a minimum, stooping to the level of liberationist, Christian-bashing bloggers and pundits is not the answer. Do not treat your opponents as they will habitually treat you—as if the merest contact with them requires a giant pair of barbecue tongs. An example of what *not* to do is the way the mainstream media tend to report on evangelicals, especially, i.e., with all the anthropological frisson of explorers encountering the Stone Age Yonomami of the Brazilian rain forest for the first time. At a minimum, those on the other side ought not follow suit.

What to do instead? For one thing, understand something that may be counterintuitive: We moderns do not really live in an age of nihilism. It is often said we do, and people in despair over what the sexual revolution and other modern changes have wrought often believe it. But contrary to such pessimists, we are not predestined by postmodernism to a nihilistic swamp—any more than the intellectuals of yesterday were predestined by Marx to a dystopian collectivist future (though many people believed that, too). In fact, people do believe in all kinds of universalizable moral codes, even if they often go by other names.

Jeane Kirkpatrick closed her "Will to Disbelieve" essay with an important point. She observed that, no matter what the reasons for the will to disbelieve may be, it is wrong simply to wash our hands of the matter and allow those in possession of bad ideas to claim a monopoly on truth. "Disbelief in the [empirical] evidence", she wrote in the context of the Cold War, "is dysfunctional. It does not correspond to the demonstrable patterns of contemporary history, and it is not, as [William] James said a true idea should be, 'profitable to our lives'."

In the end, vindication comes also comes from this fact: The intellectual divide over the Cold War and the divide today over the sexual revolution have another feature in common. In both cases, many on both sides suspected that history had already decided the matter. This was true even of some of the leading anticommunist intellectuals of the day. Jean-François Revel opened his 1984 book, chillingly entitled *How Democracies Perish*, with the equally chilling sentence: "Democracy may, after all, turn out to have been a historical accident, a brief parenthesis that is closing before our eyes."[20] Similarly, Whittaker Chambers famously opens his magisterial autobiography, *Witness*, with a letter to his children warning darkly of a world "sick unto death",[21] and he told his wife when he chose to defect from communism, "You know, we are leaving the winning world for the losing world."[22] Chambers was wrong about that, of course—even as he was singularly and fearlessly right about so much else.

---

[20] Jean-François Revel, *How Democracies Perish*, trans. William Byron (New York: Doubleday, 2004), p. 3.

[21] Whittaker Chambers, *Witness* (New York: Random House, 1952), p. 5.

[22] Ibid., p. 25.

In place of the historical materialism of those days, which seemed so towering and implacable at the time, Americans today face a different putative verdict of history: the idea that the sexual revolution is similarly a juggernaut never to be halted or reversed. That is why it is so important to get the facts right, even—or make that especially—when outnumbered by thousands to one. When people look back on this or any other momentous debate decades or centuries from now, one of the first things they will want to know is whose corner reason and empiricism and logic were in. That would be the corner of those willing to believe the truth—secured by the research of the scholars whose work testifies to it, whether the rest of the world wants to hear it or not.

2 What Is the Sexual Revolution Doing to Women?

What Does Woman Want?

One of the most fascinating aspects of the sexual revolution is that its presumed beneficiaries, upon inspection, turn out to have problems and issues that their supposedly benighted, prerevolution forebears did not. This paradox is especially evident for one rather obviously important subset of humanity: women. Let us test the proposition by way of taking as indicative certain recent lightning rods of feminine passion and ire in the U.S.

Early in 2011, sociologist Kay S. Hymowitz published an essay in the *Wall Street Journal* wondering aloud "Where Have the Good Men Gone?" The piece, based on the author's pointedly titled book *Manning Up: How the Rise of Women has Turned Men into Boys*, instantly ignited a public conflagration.[1]

Hymowitz's argument was that modern men exist in a state of suspended adolescence—even as modern women overtake them in the marketplace and elsewhere. The fundamental truth, she concluded in her tightly argued book packed with references both academic and popular, was that

[1] Kay S. Hymowitz, *Manning Up: How the Rise of Women Has Turned Men into Boys* (New York: Basic Books, 2011).

modern men and women had put themselves unwittingly on a collision course with human nature itself. "Later marriage and childbearing", she observed shrewdly, "are in an uneasy standoff with human biology, culminating in an unintended set of medical, economic, and social consequences, including more child-men, single mothers, and fatherless homes."[2]

To say that such oblique questioning of what the revolution had wrought proved controversial would be an understatement. Feminists immediately and widely deplored what they saw as blaming the women's movement for poisoning relations between the sexes. Men also attacked Hymowitz for the suggestion that so many of them spend more time with Wii and computers and video games than with the actual pursuit of live women (though many young men obviously do). Yet even more interesting than the level of passion aroused was what might be called the fact that did not bark, namely, that no one disputed Hymowitz's central point, which is that there is a unique unhappiness on today's romantic front—an important point to which we will return.

Now consider another and also highly informative public tempest from a couple of years before. For a few interesting weeks in 2009, prompted by several high-profile sex scandals, Americans following the news found themselves inundated with opinions about a particular subject: the state of marriage. From melodramas about straying Republican politicians to the separation of popular "reality show" parents Jon and Kate, the fractious state of modern marriage seemed to dominate the airwaves and blogosphere for weeks—and in its wake there floated to the surface some unusually vivid evidence of the plight of many modern women.

---

[2] Ibid., p. 176.

Just about everyone took the opportunity of these latest marital calamities to weigh in on the state of American marriage. *Newsweek* contributed a story about the rise in polyamory, that is, multiple-partner families.[3] Ruminating from Crete alongside her ex-husband and their children—pop-cultural weathervane Arianna Huffington offered another postmodern contribution: She urged other divorced parents to reach the point where "there really is nothing to work out", so that they too could vacation together as a big happy postdivorce nonfamily.[4]

Elsewhere, among other efforts to say something new about the subject, two unexpectedly compelling essays ended up serving as lightning rods: Sandra Tsing Loh's "Let's Call the Whole Thing Off" in the *Atlantic*, and Caitlin Flanagan's nearly simultaneous and ferociously opposed "Is There Hope for the American Marriage?" in *Time*.[5]

The Flanagan and Loh pieces, much more than the usual pro and con over marriage, are also windows into a rapidly evolving moral and cultural landscape. In the differences between them, ironically enough, one spies a dark albeit fascinating world of heartache for one character long said to be the prime beneficiary of the sexual revolution: modern woman.

In "Is There Hope for the American Marriage?" Flanagan took the traditionalist route, proving herself an unapologetic apologist for marriage. She staked a number

---

[3] Jessica Bennett, "Polyamory: The Next Sexual Revolution?", *Newsweek*, July 29, 2009.

[4] Arianna Huffington, "Vacationing with My Ex", *Huffington Post*, July 6, 2009, http://www.huffingtonpost.com/arianna-huffington/vacationing-with-my-ex_b_226310.html.

[5] Sandra Tsing Loh, "Let's Call the Whole Thing Off", *Atlantic*, June 29, 2009, and Caitlin Flanagan, "Is There Hope for the American Marriage?", *Time*, July 2, 2009.

of claims that have long been contested, as we have seen—among them that conventional marriage is best for children, best for adults, and critical to the success of society. Loh, on the other hand, took the opportunity of her own essay to declare herself as ferocious a foe of marriage as Flanagan was a defender of it. Using her own impending divorce as emblematic, as well as a blunt battery of anecdotes about the marriages of acquaintances and friends, Loh argued that rising lifespans and impossibly inflated expectations have ruined a once viable institution.

One obvious question—the same one at the center of Flanagan and Loh's dispute—is, what is modern marriage doing to kids? Shocking though that question proved to be to detractors of Flanagan's *Time* essay, not everyone is so naive; readers passably acquainted with the decades of family sociology following the Moynihan Report will already suspect the answer. More interesting is another question: What is modern marriage doing to adults? More precisely, what today is the state, in our apparently postmodern, postfeminist, postjudgmental social order, of what antiquarians once thought of as "the war between the sexes"?

The answer seems to be one long, strange trip to an enigma in which many unhappy people apparently feel themselves trapped.

"Let's Call the Whole Thing Off" is a searing, sometimes brutal, attack on traditional marriage. It could also fairly be called postfeminist, in that its chief complaint is not so much that men are intolerable as that marriage per se is impossible. Loh's essay marches relentlessly through the details of her own marital collapse (initiated by the author herself, as she acknowledges from the outset), her itinerant misgivings about what the split might do to her children, and her conversations with friends and others that further fuel her thesis. "Now that we have white-collar work and washing machines and a life expectancy that has shot from forty-seven to seventy-seven", she argues, the idea of marriage "has become obsolete". The essay closes with a "final piece of advice" that delivers its gist with bitter élan: "Avoid marriage—or you too may suffer the emotional pain, the humiliation, and the logistical difficulty, not to mention the expense, of breaking up a long-term union at midlife for something as demonstrably fleeting as love."[6]

Meanwhile, Flanagan undertook a pithy channeling of what generations of social scientists have been painstakingly documenting since the 1960s: "There is no other single force causing as much measurable hardship and human misery in this country as the collapse of marriage. It hurts children, it reduces mothers' financial security, and it has landed with particular devastation on those who can bear it least: the nation's underclass." Citing just a handful of some of the authors who have been putting out the bad news about broken homes for years (including those cited in the preceding chapter of this book)—among them Robert Rector, David Blankenhorn, and Sara McLanahan—Flanagan excoriated her happy-talking divorcing or unmarried peers with children for their willful blindness. Reaching even beyond the defense of marriage to a warning about the wider social ramifications of the collapse of the family, she concluded on a note plainly designed to chill her fellow baby boomers above all: "The current generation of children, the one watching commitments between adults snap like dry twigs and observing parents who simply can't be bothered to marry each other and who hence drift in and out of their children's lives—that's

[6] Sandra Tsing Loh, "Let's Call the Whole Thing Off", *Atlantic Magazine* July/August 2009, http://www.theatlantic.com/magazine/archive/2009/07/let-8217-s-call-the-whole-thing-off/7488/.

the generation who will be taking care of us when we are old."[7]

If the authors didn't exactly pussyfoot around their theses, neither did the commentators rushing to pummel them. Flanagan, predictably enough, was roundly flogged by the usual suspects for what her sophisticated critics correctly interpret as a shockingly retrograde defense of the family—one all the more unusual because, unlike most other champions of heterosexual marriage in the public square these days, Flanagan is a supporter of abortion who relies largely on anecdote and occasional secular sociology to make her case.

This narrative novelty, far from sparing her the wrath of her critics, seems instead to have inflamed it exponentially. Blasting even in advance of the appearance of the *Time* essay, alpha feminist Linda Hirshman derided its author as a "working-mother scourge", complained of her reliance on "outmoded studies" and "interviews with experts from right-wing foundations", and ultimately excoriated *Time* itself for "running another unsubstantiated, apocalyptic cover on the awful consequences of most American women's fates".[8]

Writing in the *Nation*, populist feminist Katha Pollitt sharpened similar claws Dubbing Flanagan a "professional anti-feminist" and "author of a whole book of essays attacking working mothers, herself excepted", she concluded that "the attack on divorce isn't really about poor people and their families", but about "reinforcing the idea that 'the family'

[7] Caitlin Flanagan, "Is There Hope for the American Marriage?", *Time Magazine*, July 2, 2009, http://www.time.com/time/magazine/article/0,9171,1908434,00.html.

[8] Linda Hirshman, "Only Caitlin Flanagan Could Make Mark Sanford Look Good", guest post, *XX Factor*, July 2, 2009, http://www.slate.com/blogs/xx_factor/2009/07/02/caitlin_flanagan_makes_mark_sanford_look_good.htm.

is not just a haven in a heartless world but the only safety net you have, or should have, from the blows of fortune"[9]— apparently, to those of Pollitt's way of thinking, about as ludicrous an idea as can be imagined. Across the progressive-left side of the spectrum, commentators agreed in similarly excoriating Flanagan for what most regarded as one more retrograde defense of the indefensible nuclear family.

Sandra Tsing Loh, not surprisingly, got off more leniently in the same quarters for her confession of an affair and her subsequent decision to divorce. Though some readers wrote the piece off in disgust, others sympathized and openly applauded her move, albeit with occasional qualifications. "No doubt," as a writer at *Salon* put it, "some will blame Loh for not trying hard enough. But she's never been one to show us the ideal; just what's real."[10] Left-wing blogger Amanda Marcotte, another indicator, echoed Loh in a piece titled (with admirable clarity): "For Many, Marriage Is Sexless, Boring, and Oppressive: Time to Rethink the Institution?"[11]

One intriguing fact unmentioned in the general fray was that Loh's portrayal *did* draw consistent demurral from at least one subset of readers: men. Delving at some length into the essay and its author for the *Los Angeles Times*, James Rainey criticized the implication that today's married men are "disdained by their wives as being less than men. These twenty-first-century pantywaists follow all the new rules—providing incomes, helping with parenting, sharing chores,

---

[9] Katha Pollitt, "Can This Marriage Be Saved?", *Nation*, August 3, 2009, http://www.thenation.com/article/can-marriage-be-saved-1.

[10] Amy Benfer, "When 'Date Night' Is Not Enough", *Salon*, June 18, 2009, http://www.salon.com/2009/06/18/loh_on_divorce/.

[11] Amanda Marcotte, "For Many, Marriage Is Sexless, Boring, and Oppressive: Time to Rethink the Institution?", *AlterNet*, July 1, 2009, http://www.alternet.org/sex/141024/?cID=1250426.

and cooking elaborate meals—and in the process become domesticated, sexless drones."[12] A blogger at MensNews-Daily.com dismissed the essay as "the same self-absorbed mewling we see periodically from the privileged", as the author's "desperate attempt to explain herself to herself (and unfortunately, to us)". Other male critics, though few females, similarly faulted Loh for her generalization of today's married man as a sexless, sex-withholding "competitor wife".[13]

What to make of this unexpected but telling tempest in a summer teapot, one so emblematic of the state of romance today?

On the intellectual playing field, of course, Flanagan—like Hymowitz and others who read the evidence with honest eyes—got everything right, beginning with the not insignificant libraries of social science now testifying to the effects of broken homes on children. So many economists, sociologists, psychologists, and other experts have by now contributed to that record that no single set of books, let alone a *Time* essay of a few thousand words, can hope to capture it, but Flanagan did about as well with the challenge as anyone has.

Even so—and here is where things begin to get curiouser—the 2009 summer marriage wars went deeper than a mere empirical slam dunk about kids and broken homes. In the depth and rawness of much commentary there lurked a different kind of truth telling that went largely undiscussed—what might even be called an inadvertent form of truth telling about just how lost a great many modern people, especially

[12] James Rainey, "Sandra Tsing Loh Reveals Affair and Anti-Marriage Stance", *Los Angeles Times*, June 17, 2009, http://articles.latimes.com/2009/jun/17/entertainment/et-onthemedia17.

[13] Robert Franklin, "Lipotrex without Prescription", *Glenn Sacks* (blog), July 2, 2009, http://glennsacks.com/blog/?p-3928.

women, are today. As the peerless Midge Decter once noted, "the real truth about the sexual revolution is that it has made of sex an almost chaotically limitless and therefore unmanageable realm in the life of women." [14] It is an insight to which the summer 2009 marriage war, like the 2011 controversy over *Manning Up*, stands as a large footnote.

Yet there is more to be mined here in the effort to understand just how some of the revolution's supposed beneficiaries also became its victims. Today's revolution against traditional marriage amounts to two charges made repeatedly, almost always by women and with many echoes elsewhere in contemporary sources: first, that the combined pressures of motherhood and marriage and breadwinning are just too much to bear; and second, that many of today's marriages—that is to say, marriages made among enlightened, older, educated, sophisticated people—are a sexual desert. It is almost as if the war between the sexes has ended: first, in the figurative sense that there are no more sexes, only lists of chores that one gender unit mysteriously does better than the other; and second, in the literal sense that there are no more sexes—because contemporary man, many contemporary women charge, has lost interest in sex.

This complaint—that today's husbands, at least of the enlightened, chore-sharing variety, can be counted on to lose interest in sex with their wives—is so central to Loh's essay, for example, that the piece might accurately have been subtitled "A Manifesto against Metrosexuals". In her judgment, this common misery amounts to a social trend—including among many of her friends, even those with marriages that might appear ideal. "When marriage was

---

[14] Midge Decter, *The New Chastity and Other Arguments against Women's Liberation* (New York: Perigee, 1974), p. 80.

invented," she quoted another friend whose husband has also allegedly lost all interest in sex, "it was considered to be a kind of trade union for a woman, her protection against the sexually wandering male. But what's happened to the sexually wandering male?" As Loh summarized, "To work, to parent, to housekeep, to be the ones who schedule 'date night', only to be reprimanded in the home by male kitchen bitches, and then, in the bedroom, to be ignored—it's a bum deal."[15]

To certain of these specifics, interestingly enough, Caitlin Flanagan and her allies on the other side would almost certainly agree. Writing in the *Atlantic* several years ago about "The Wifely Duty", she made similar points about modern man and woman.[16] Citing a variety of sources—sex therapists, popular novels, friends, and correspondents—she reflected at length on the portrait painted by Loh: Many modern marriages, at least in the more stylish circles being reported on, are sexually barren. As no less an authority than Dr. Phil put it, "Sexless marriages are an undeniable epidemic." A sizeable industry of therapists and other experts has lately risen to what surely would have seemed an odd vocation to most preceding generations, namely, teaching married people how to have sex.

This brings us to a third example of reports about the unique unhappiness about today's romantic scene, at least for some. The complaint that there is something uniquely dissatisfying—that is, sexually dissatisfying—about modern marriage turns out to have been plumbed ubiquitously of late, at least by women. In yet another essay about yet another therapist, published by yet another

---

[15] Loh, *Atlantic Magazine* (see chap. 2, n. 6).

[16] Caitlin Flanagan, "The Wifely Duty", *Atlantic*, January–February 2003.

female writer for the *Atlantic,* Cristina Nehring similarly pondered the question of sexlessness, only to decide:

> We are talking ourselves to death. We are talking our desire to death.... Perhaps we could regain some of sexuality's transgressive energy by *re*mystifying our eroticism rather than by *de*mystifying it, by re*veil*ing our desire rather than by rehearsing it ad nauseam, by rediscovering the power of wit and suggestion, sublimation and caesura.[17]

Other writers plumbing this new confessional mode have similarly drawn attention to the demise of romance not only in marriage but in all relations between men and women. The utter boredom even figures into the justifications for polyamory offered by a couple of proponents in the *Newsweek* piece. "I think if we were all given a choice, everyone would choose some form of open relationship", one observed. "I just like variety", another agrees. "I get bored!"[18]

Is there nonanecdotal evidence out there that this latest form of female dissatisfaction amounts to more than just another example of certain people spending more time on the Internet than they probably should? Yes, and plenty of it.

In 2009, most notably, two Wharton School economists, Betsey Stevenson and Justin Wolfers, called forth considerable comment with their groundbreaking and much commented–upon paper on the subject, "The Paradox of Declining Female Happiness".[19] Using thirty-five years of

[17] Cristina Nehring, "Of Sex and Marriage", *Atlantic,* December 2006, http://www.theatlantic.com/magazine/archive/2006/12/of-sex-and-marriage/5373/.

[18] Jessica Bennett, "Polyamory: The Next Sexual Revolution?", *Newsweek,* July 29, 2009, http://www.thedailybeast.com/newsweek/2009/07/28/only-you-and-you-and-you.html.

[19] Betsey Stevenson and Justin Wolfers, "The Paradox of Declining Female Happiness", *American Economic Journal: Economic Policy* 1, no. 2 (2009): 190–225.

data from the General Social Survey, they observe that, given the many social and economic transformations of modernity that would appear to benefit women—a closing gender wage gap, an educational attainment that now tops that of men, the sexual freedom conveyed by artificial contraception, and more—one would reasonably expect to see those who are the beneficiaries of these trends registering increased happiness.

Instead—and hence the paradox of the study's title—the reverse seems to be true: Over the past thirty-five years, "women's happiness has fallen both absolutely and relative to men's in a pervasive way among groups, such that women no longer report being happier than men and, in many instances, now report happiness that is below that of men." Moreover, their data show, "this shift has occurred through much of the industrialized world." [20]

So what is happening out there to account for all these miserable, dissatisfied wives and mothers? Why are many of today's marriages apparently peopled by snippy, ineffectual husbands and smoldering (in all senses) desperate housewives?

Part of the answer appears to be, first, that many marriages are *not* like that. At the same time, given the vivid testimony to the contrary of so many contemporary women, there is no denying that at least some of the dissatisfaction they describe—specifically, the dissatisfaction among enlightened, upper-middle-class, university-educated interchangeable gender and work partners—is all too real.

One explanation for this rise in domestic misery that is currently making the rounds is longevity. Of course, it is difficult to take seriously an argument that so perversely turns a good thing (longer life) into a bad one (unwanted

---

[20] Ibid., abstract, p. 190.

extra years of marriage). But even if we did—to draw a parallel to the point made by those Wharton economists—any unhappiness at being stuck more years with a partner ought to be more than offset by a few other benefits that the health revolution has wrought: drastically lower infant- and child-mortality rates, far less incidence of death in child-birth, and the like. So the simple fact that we are all living longer—at least the fortunate among us—seems hardly to explain today's increased female immiseration.

Another answer proposed lately may get closer to the heart of the matter. In widely discussed research published in 2009, psychologist Jean Twenge used data collected from some sixteen thousand college students and found a sharp rise in scores on a "narcissism index" personality test among young adults—disproportionately, among the young women.[21] (In the 1950s, to take one example from the index, only 12 per-cent of college students agreed that "I am an important per-son", whereas that figure was 80 percent by the late 1980s.)[22] This "narcissism epidemic", as some have termed it, has in turn given rise to speculation about what might account for such an exaggerated sense of oneself: Capitalism? Indulgent, ego-pampering parenting? Digital technology that relent-lessly raises the bar for personal appearance?

While the jury of psychologists remains out, the charge of narcissism does seem convincing, as reading just a few hundred of the assorted essays, blogs, and other public com-plaints entered in the "new confessional mode" makes pain-fully clear. Throw in also, for those who can bear it, the booming subgenre of contemporary books deriding chil-dren and domesticity with tellingly ugly titles like *The Bitch*

[21] Jean M. Twenge and W. Keith Campbell, *The Narcissism Epidemic: Living in the Age of Entitlement* (New York: Free Press, 2009).
[22] Ibid, p. 34.

in the House and *Bad Mother* and others too depressing even to catalogue. Today's resentment of domesticity is not the hate that has no name; it is the hate that won't shut up. It emanates from the self-same women who are, after all, among the most historically fortunate members of their sex in world history, which does suggest something deranged about the whole dynamic. If this is not psychotic narcissism in the clinical sense, there is at least abundant pop-literary evidence of a uniquely spoiled and ungrateful age.

Even so, dismissing this ongoing new outcry of feminine injury would be a mistake—because, annoying and risible though it may appear, there is an unmistakable authenticity running through it. Some of these writers may really be onto something, though it seems not to be something that most of them want to face.

Nevertheless, clues abound for those with eyes to see. Back in her 2003 essay on "The Wifely Duty", for example, Caitlin Flanagan discerned that ideologically imposed sexlessness is obviously part of the problem. She observed,

> What we've learned during this thirty-year grand experiment is that men can be cajoled into doing all kinds of household tasks, but they will not do them the way a woman would.... They will, in other words, do as men have always done: reduce a job to its simplest essentials and utterly ignore the fillips and niceties that women tend to regard as equally essential. And a lot of women feel cheated and angry and even—bless their hearts—surprised about this.

Similarly, Kay Hymowitz has emphasized the dissonance induced by women's demands for equal treatment in the boardroom, the clubs, the playing fields—everywhere but in matters of romance.

They are undoubtedly right about domesticities and double standards. Women have higher standards than men about most of the realities of housekeeping and spend more time on them.[23] The linguistic innovations devised to reflect our new domestic world alone go to show as much. Women who work outside the home, for instance, have a "second shift", though men do not. Likewise, there is a reason the phrase "having it all" is used only about modern woman—because only a modern woman would attempt so many tasks at once. No man would drive himself mad trying to *pretend* he'd baked a pie—to take an example from the celebrated opening scene of a lighter look at the war between the sexes, Allison Pearson's 2002 novel, *I Don't Know How She Does It.*[24]

Yet the explanation from imposed gender neutrality does not by itself go far enough. Something else lurks under the rocks picked up by the fashionable writing about marriage these days—something that crawls away from the light even as it squirms just under the surface of much of the new confessionalism. In particular, judging by various sources, pornography is the invisible ink of many of these essays and lives—obvious one minute, unnoticed the next, and the bearer of a message no one apparently sees. Understood or not, however, it appears to be leaving a mark on at least some of these publicly lived lives.

In Loh's essay, for example, a husband—as it happens, one of those husbands no longer interested in sex with his wife—bookmarks his pornography on the computer. His wife knows all about it, even reporting it to her friends who are also

[23] See, for example, Judith Treas and Sonia Drobnic, eds., *Dividing the Domestic: Men, Women and Household Work in Cross-National Perspective* (Stanford, Calif.: Stanford University Press, 2010).

[24] Allison Pearson, *I Don't Know How She Does It: The Life of Kate Reddy, Working Mother* (New York: Knopf, 2002).

commiserating about their sexless marriages. Yet no one seems to connect these possible causal dots at all. Another blogger for *Salon*, reflecting on Loh's essay, similarly nudged up against this obvious if missing piece of the puzzle (in a piece called "Why Your Marriage Sucks"), noting, "I write this article from a hotel room in New York City, where nearly a dozen porn movies are on offer"—a fact the author uses to highlight what she thinks of as an irony, when it might instead suggest something else: a possible and in fact rather obvious link between all those movies on the one hand and, on the other hand, a loss of romantic interest on the part of those who think them inconsequential.[25]

Or consider the critical success of a successful 2007 chick-lit book by author Joan Sewell called *I'd Rather Eat Chocolate*.[26] Praised in *Salon* and the *Atlantic* and other cutting-edge venues, it is the casually told story of a husband and wife whose tension over marital sex leads finally to an amicable solution: She has her chocolate, and he has his Internet pornography. Once again, might there just be a connection between all this casual talk (and use) of pornography—and all those frustrated women and disinterested husbands?

So why does Dr. Phil and every run-of-the-mill pastor in America understand what so many unhappy women apparently do not? The answer is that the kind of feminism these women have so unthinkingly imbibed has come at a great cost. It has rendered many of them ideologically if not personally blasé about something they cannot really afford to be blasé about. In her widely noted 2005 manifesto called *Female Chauvinist Pigs: Women and the Rise of Raunch Culture*,

---

[25] Amanda Fortini, "Why Your Marriage Sucks", *Salon*, June 24, 2009, http://www.salon.com/2009/06/24/vindication_love/.

[26] Joan Sewall, *I'd Rather Eat Chocolate: Learning to Love My Low Libido* (New York: Crown Archetype, 2007).

writer Ariel Levy chronicles the steady infiltration of pornography into female society.[27] The pressure on women to accept pornography as an inconsequential and entertaining fact of life rises steadily—and outside the circles of the conservative and the religious, there is little cultural ammunition for any woman who wants to resist it.

In fact, one of the few other tony writers who does seem to grasp the destructive role of pornography in modern romance is "third wave" feminist Naomi Wolf. Author of numerous excruciatingly frank books about her own life as a daughter of the sexual revolution (one candidly titled *Promiscuities*), Wolf is no one's idea of a traditionalist, morally or otherwise. Yet she has also been willing to see and say about smut certain truths that her ideological allies will not. In a particularly controversial essay published in *New York* magazine in 2003, for example, she chillingly observed that "the onslaught of porn is responsible for deadening male libido in relation to real women, and leading men to see fewer and fewer women as porn-worthy." [28] It is a theme that continues to preoccupy her. In 2011, following the excruciating public implosion of a congressman in a texting-and-sexting scandal, Wolf observed that "many highly visible men in recent years ... have behaved in sexually destructive ways", which led her to ask, "Is Porn Driving Men Crazy?" [29] It is a curious fact telling us much about where the revolution has left us that almost none of her feminist sisters have followed suit.

[27] Ariel Levy, *Female Chauvinist Pigs: Women and the Rise of Raunch Culture* (New York: Free Press, 2005).

[28] Naomi Wolf, "The Porn Myth", *New York*, October 20, 2003, http://nymag.com/nymetro/news/trends/n_9437/.

[29] Naomi Wolf, "Is Porn Driving Men Crazy?", *Project Syndicate*, June 30, 2011, http://www.project-syndicate.org/commentary/wolf37/English.

All of which brings us back to the question of what women really want. In the postrevolutionary world, sex is easier had than ever before; but the opposite appears true for romance. This is perhaps the central enigma that modern men and women are up against: romantic want in a time of sexual plenty. Perhaps some of the modern misery of which so many women today so authentically speak is springing not from a sexual desert, but from a sexual flood— a torrent of poisonous imagery, beginning now for many in childhood, that has engulfed women and men, only to beach them eventually somewhere alone and apart, far from the reach of one another.

At least that way of looking at the puzzle might explain some of the paradox of all that female unhappiness. Between bad ideas of gender neutrality and even worse ideas of the innocence of pornography, we reach the world so vividly described by so many dissatisfied women today, one where men act like stereotypical women, and retreat from real relationships into a fantasy life via pornography (rather than Harlequin novels), and where women conversely act like stereotypical men, taking the lead in leaving their marriages and firing angry charges on the way, out of frustration and withheld sex.

It was not supposed to happen that way, but it has. Enlightened people following the sexual revolution only meant to take the small-*s* sex out of marriage: the unwanted gender division. But along the way, capital-*s* Sex appears to have headed for the exits along with it, at least for a vocal and embittered minority. This lack of sexual intimacy in a world awash in sexual imagery is worth meditating upon for a moment—which raises the next obvious question before us, which is what the revolution has meant for another nonnegligible subset of the population: men.

3 What Is the Sexual Revolution Doing to Men?

Peter Pan and the Weight of Smut

The number of blogs, columns, books, essays, and articles in recent years dissecting the perpetual adolescence of the American male is far too high to count—as is the even higher number of e-mails, texts, women's television shows, and porch conversations dedicated to that same theme. Ubiquitously, it seems, those who were once husbands and fathers and providers have traded in their ties and insurance cards for video games and baseball hats worn backwards. It is a message that the popular culture also broadcasts nonstop—from vehicles for women like *Sex in the City* and *The View* to those popular among men, including such commercially successful examples as the *Jackass* franchise, the Spike channel, and just about every comedy about idiot males to issue from Hollywood in recent memory.

Even so, the question of why this sea change has come about has for the most part escaped critical attention—with a few notable exceptions. In a searching essay written several years ago, for example, Joseph Epstein analyzed "The Perpetual Adolescent and the Triumph of the Youth Culture", ultimately attributing the phenomenon to postwar prosperity; "[e]arlier," he theorized, "with less money around,

people were forced to get serious, to grow up—and fast." [1]
In 2007, Diana West considered the same question in her
forthrightly titled book *The Death of the Grown-Up: How
America's Arrested Development Is Bringing Down Western Civilization*.[2] Like Epstein, she cited affluence as one cause, add-
ing also the sexual revolution and a generalized vanishing
of adult standards of conduct. Kay S. Hymowitz, in her
previously mentioned 2011 book *Manning Up*, offered another
nuanced answer, citing women's higher performance in education and a job market requiring more years of schooling
as causal factors in the rise of the "child-man".

Yet while these and like-minded thinkers have obviously
each got a part of the truth, it is surely the sexual revolution that is the prime mover of the phenomenon they all
describe. This seems so for at least two reasons. First, it has
led to an atrophying of the protective instinct in many men—
because many have nothing to protect. The powerful majority desire for recreative rather than procreative sex has led
not only to a marriage dearth, but also to a birth dearth;
and as the old saying correctly goes, "Adults don't make
babies; babies make adults."

Second, and as a related matter, what might be called the
consumerization of love—the way that many people now
go shopping for sex and romance much as they do for inan-
imate commodities—has had a rather major unintended consequence. It has led to more discerning consumers in an
area of life where heightened discernment appears inimical
to long-term satisfaction. In other words, the perpetual and

[1] Joseph Epstein, "The Perpetual Adolescent and the Triumph of the Youth
Culture", *Weekly Standard*, March 15, 2004, http://www.weeklystandard.com/
content/public/articles/000/000/003/825grtdi.asp.

[2] Diana West, *The Death of the Grown-Up: How America's Arrested Development Is Bringing Down Western Civilization* (New York: St. Martin's Press, 2007).

often successful hunt for sexual novelty ultimately works to the detriment of longer-term romance. This is nowhere as obvious as in recent research on another aspect of the child-man of today: his use of smut, or what might otherwise be called the paradox of declining male happiness in an age glutted by sexual imagery.

Let us approach this paradox by way of an analogy. As any number of impressively depressing cover stories have lately served to remind us all, the weight-gain epidemic in the United States and the rest of the West is indeed widespread, deleterious, and unhealthy—which is why it is so frequently remarked on, and an object of such universal public concern. But while America is on the subject of bad habits that can turn unwitting kids into unhappy adults, how about that other epidemic out there that is far more likely to make their future lives miserable than carrying those extra pounds ever will? That would be the emerging social phenomenon of what can appropriately be called "sexual obesity": the widespread gorging on pornographic imagery that is also deleterious and unhealthy, though far less remarked on than that other epidemic—and nowhere near an object of universal public concern.

The term "sexual obesity" comes from Mary Ann Layden, a psychiatrist who runs the Sexual Trauma and Psychopathology Program at the University of Pennsylvania. She sees the victims of Internet-pornography consumption in her practice, day in and day out. She also knows what most do not: Quietly, patiently, and irrefutably, an empirical record of the harms of sexual obesity is being assembled piecemeal via the combined efforts of psychologists, sociologists, addiction specialists, psychiatrists, and other authorities.

Young people who have been exposed to pornography are more likely to have multiple lifetime sexual partners, more likely to have had more than one sexual partner in the last three months, more likely to have used alcohol or other substances at their last sexual encounter, and—no surprise here—more likely to have scored higher on a "sexual permissiveness" test. They are also more likely to have tried risky forms of sex. They are also more likely to engage in forced sex and more likely to be sexual offenders. As for the all-purpose cop-out that "all this shows is correlation", it can be refuted as Dr. Johnson famously refuted the immaterialism of Bishop Berkeley—by kicking a stone. No one who is reasonable would doubt that there is a connection between watching sex acts and trying out what one sees—especially for adolescents, who rather famously and instantly ape the other influences on their lives, from fashion to drug use and more, as has also been copiously studied by academic experts and nervous parents alike throughout the ages.

And this list is just one possible way of starting a conversation about the consequences of the novel obesity that the sugary smut of the Internet has induced. There is also the question of what the same material does to adults—about which another empirical record is also being amassed. Pornography today, in short, is much like obesity was yesterday—a social problem increasing over time, with especially worrisome results among its youngest consumers, and one whose harms are only beginning to be studied with the seriousness they clearly deserve.

The parallels between the two epidemics are striking. Much like the more commonly understood obesity, the phenomenon of sexual obesity permeates the population—though unlike regular obesity, of course, pornography consumption is mostly (though not entirely) a male thing. At the same time, evidence also shows that sexual obesity does share with its counterpart this critical common denominator: It afflicts the subset of human beings who form the first generation immersed in this consumption, many of whom have never known a world without it—the young.

Consider some of the newly available data about the immersion of young Americans in pornography. One 2008 study focused on undergraduate and graduate students ages eighteen to twenty-six across the country found that more than two-thirds of men—and one out of every ten women in the sample—viewed pornography more than once a month.[3] Another study, in the *Journal of Adolescent Health*, showed that first-year college students using sexually explicit material exhibited these features: increased tolerance, resulting in a turn toward more bizarre and esoteric material; increased risk of body-image problems, especially among girls; and erroneous and exaggerated conceptions of how prevalent certain sexual behaviors, including risky-to-dangerous behaviors, actually are.[4]

In 2004, the National Center on Addiction and Substance Abuse at Columbia University reported that 65 percent of boys ages sixteen and seventeen reported having friends who regularly download Internet pornography[5]—and, given that pornography is something people lie "down"

[3] J. S. Carroll et al., "Generation XXX: Pornography Acceptance and Use among Emerging Adults", *Journal of Adolescent Research* 23, no. 1 (2008): 6–30.

[4] D. Zillman, "Influence of Unrestrained Access to Erotica on Adolescents' and Young Adults' Dispositions toward Sexuality", *Journal of Adolescent Health* 27 (2000): 41–44.

[5] The National Center on Addiction and Substance Abuse at Columbia University, "National Survey of American Attitudes on Subsance Abuse IX: Teen Dating Practices and Sexual Activity", August 2004, p. 6. For a summary see C. C. Radsch, "Teenagers' Sexual Activity Is Tied to Drugs and Drink", *New York Times*, August 20, 2004, p. A14.

about in surveys as well as in life, it seems safe to say those numbers underestimate today's actual consumption, perhaps even significantly. And to connect the dots between "monkey see" and "monkey do", a 2004 study in *Pediatrics* conducted by several researchers from the Rand Corporation and the University of California at Santa Barbara reported, in the words of its title, that "Watching Sex on Television Predicts Adolescent Initiation of Sexual Behavior"—surely a problematic finding for anyone wanting to argue that we are not much influenced by what we see.[6]

Of course all the social science data now accumulating cannot answer a question almost as ubiquitous as pornography itself: So what? Why should people who are not part of that consumption even care about it? Pornography indeed may be wrong, many of those people would also say (and of course major religions would agree), but, apart from the possible damage to the user's soul, if you even believe in such a thing, what really is the social harm of smut?

This lackadaisical attitude—this entrenched refusal to look seriously at what the computer screen has really wrought—is widespread. Religious people, among other people simply disgusted by the subject, understandably wish to speak in public of almost anything else. Consumers of pornography will probably already have stopped reading these words—or any others potentially critical of their chosen substance—for reasons of their own; such complicity is probably the deepest font of omertà on the subject. And chronic users above all have their own fierce reasons for promoting the

---

[6] Rebecca L. Collins et al., "Watching Sex on Television Predicts Adolescent Initiation of Sexual Behavior", *Pediatrics* 114, no. 3 (September 2004): e280–e289.

anything-goes-as-long-as-it's-private patter—an interesting
phenomenon about which more will be said further on.

And yet this hands-off approach to the matter of sexual
obesity—this unwitting collusion of disparate interested parties masquerading as a social consensus—remains wrong.
Consider a 2009 document signed by fifty academic and
other authorities representing various fields and distilling
just some of the recent empirical evidence.[7] Called "The
Social Costs of Pornography: A Statement of Findings and
Recommendations", it is not the work of one or two but
rather scores of people. Most of them academics and medical professionals, they represent a true rainbow coalition of
the spectrum: left and right, feminism and conservatism,
secularism, Judaism, Christianity, and Islam. It is a collec-
tive attempt to render for the public good just some of the
accumulating academic and therapeutic and other evidence
of the harm and devastation now traceable to pornography
abuse.

Bursting through the academically neutral language of the
report—the studies, the survey data, the econometrics and
the rest—were the skin and bones of the very human stories that went into it all: the marriages lost or in tatters; the
sexual problems among the addicted; the constant slide, on
account of higher tolerance, into ever edgier circles of this
hell; the children and teenagers lured into participating in
various ways in this awful world in the effort to please romantic partners or exploitive adults. This report, in sum, like
the conference that preceded it, answers definitively the libertarian question of "So what about pornography?" with a
solid list of "Here's what"—eight documented findings about

[7] Full disclosure: the document in question, "The Social Costs of Pornography: A Statement of Findings and Recommendations", was co-drafted
by Mary Ann Layden and me (Princeton, N.J.: Witherspoon Institute, 2010).

the risks of warping the sexual template with pornographic imagery.

Of all the untruths about this subject today that are belied by the factual record, let us focus here on just three of the most influential and reckless.

Pornography use is just a private matter. Perhaps the queen bee of lies about the subject, this is also the easiest to take down. For while *consumption* of the substance may be private (or not, as airline travelers and library patrons and others in the public square have lately been learning), the fallout from some of that consumption is anything but.

Consider just a few examples from recent studies on people younger than eighteen. Several separate studies have found among adolescents a strong correlation between pornography consumption and engaging in various sexual activities. Adolescent users of pornography are more likely to intend to have sex, to have sex earlier, and to engage in more frequent sexual activity.[8] The exceedingly well-documented social costs of adolescent sexual activity, alongside the health costs now accumulating, alone torpedo the refrain that Internet pornography use today is "private".

Now consider a few more findings concerning adults rather than adolescents. At a November 2003 meeting of the American Academy of Matrimonial Lawyers (comprising the nation's top 1,600 divorce and matrimonial-law attorneys),

[8] More likely to intend to have sex: see K. L. L'Engle, J. Brown, and K. Kenneavy, "The Mass Media Are an Important Context for Adolescents' Sexual Behavior", *Journal of Adolescent Health* 38, no. 4, (2006): 186–92. Earlier initiation: J. Brown and K. L'Engle, "X-Rated: Sexual Attitudes and Behaviors Associated with U.S. Early Adolescents' Exposure to Sexually Explicit Media", *Communication Research* 36 (2009): 129–51. Having sexual activity more frequently: L'Engle et al., "Mass Media". See also G. Wingood et al., "Exposure to X-Rated Movies and Adolescents' Sexual and Contraceptive Related Attitudes and Behaviors", *Pediatrics* 107, no. 5 (2001): 1116–19.

62 percent of the 350 attendees said the Internet had played a role in divorces during the last year.[9] Divorce, as everyone knows by now, is associated with a variety of adverse financial and other outcomes as well as with problems for children and adolescents affected by it. To the extent that pornography use increases the likelihood of marital breakup, such private behavior is clearly exacting public costs.

Pornography use is a guy thing. It only bothers women. In fact, some of the saddest and most riveting testimony on this topic concerns exactly this: the harm that pornography consumption can do to men immersed in it.

Consider the research of Pamela Paul, a former reporter for *Time* magazine, who interviewed in depth more than one hundred heterosexual users of pornography—80 percent of them men—for her 2005 book *Pornified: How Pornography Is Transforming Our Lives, Our Relationships, and Our Families.*[10] This book—the best yet written in laymen's terms about the impact of Internet pornography on users themselves—is remarkable for several reasons. Just one is the unforgettably sad portrait that emerges, sometimes unwittingly, from habitual users themselves. "Countless men", she summarizes from the interviews, "have described to me how, while using pornography, they have lost the ability to relate to or be close to women. They have trouble being turned on by 'real' women, and their sex lives with their girlfriends or wives collapse."[11]

---

[9] Reported by Pamela Paul, "The Porn Factor", *Time*, January 29, 2004.

[10] Pamela Paul, *Pornified: How Pornography Is Transforming Our Lives, Our Relationships, and Our Families* (New York: Times Books, 2005).

[11] Pamela Paul, "From Pornography to Porno to Porn: How Porn Became the Norm", in *The Social Cost of Pornography: A Collection of Papers*, ed. James R. Stoner Jr. and Donna M. Hughes (Princeton, N.J.: Witherspoon Institute, 2010), p. 6.

The same point has been echoed by medical authorities, including Norman Doidge, a doctor specializing in neuropsychiatry and author of *The Brain That Changes Itself: Stories of Personal Triumph from the Frontiers of Brain Science.*[12] Treating men in the early to mid-1990s for their pornography habits, he found it a common refrain that many were no longer able to have intercourse with their own wives. "Pornographers", he concludes, "promise healthy pleasure and relief from sexual tension, but what they often deliver is an addiction, tolerance, and an eventual decrease in pleasure. Paradoxically, the male patients I worked with often craved pornography but didn't like it." [13]

But self-loathing is hardly limited to the most extreme cases. In 2010, the widely followed conservative website *National Review Online* ran an anonymous and widely discussed piece called "Getting Serious about Pornography". Its author, a mother of five, detailed and deplored pornography's role as she saw it in the destruction of her marriage. The result was an outpouring of impassioned e-mail—including from some people exploring their own use of pornography and its impact on their own lives. Perhaps most poignant of all was the testimony of users themselves whose lives had been made miserable by the stuff.

As Roger Scruton has put the paradox about men and pornography memorably, "This, it seems to me, is the real risk attached to pornography. Those who become addicted to this risk-free form of sex run a risk of another and greater

[12] Norman Doidge, *The Brain That Changes Itself: Stories of Personal Triumph from the Frontiers of Brain Science* (New York: Viking Adult, 2007).
[13] Ibid., p. 48.

kind. They risk the loss of love, in a world where only love brings happiness." [14]

It's only pictures of consenting adults. Unless it is computer simulated, pornography is never only about pictures. Every single person on the screen is somebody's sister, cousin, son, niece, or mother; every one of them stands in a human relation to the world.

The notion for starters that those in the "industry" itself are not being harmed by what they do cannot survive even the briefest reading of testimonials to the contrary by those who have turned their backs on it. It is a world rife with everything one would want any genuinely loved one to avoid like the plague: drugs, exploitation, physical harm, AIDS.

Nor can the "pictures" defense survive the extremely troubling—or what ought to be extremely troubling— connections between pornography and prostitution. What is now called "sex trafficking", for example, is often associated with pornography—for example, via cameras and film equipment found when trafficking circles are broken up. Plainly, the reality of the human beings behind many of those images on the Internet is poorer, dirtier, druggier— and younger—than pious appeals to "consenting adults" can withstand.

Perhaps somewhere among our public crusaders against "regular" obesity, there will emerge a person of stature who can spare time for this other epidemic, too. After all, uninviting though these dirty waters may be, the reward for tackling this epidemic could be profound. For amid the squalor,

---

[14] Roger Scruton, "The Abuse of Sex", in *The Social Costs of Pornography: A Collection of Papers*, ed. James R. Stoner Jr. and Donna M. Hughes (Princeton, N.J.: Witherspoon Institute, 2010), p. 125.

the unhappiness, and the rest of the bad news about sexual obesity, the bad news is not the only news there is—not at all.

"Where sin increased," as Paul's Letter to the Romans has it, "grace abounded all the more" (5:20). The record of what pornography has wrought shows that kind of abundance too, though it may not yet be an issue of academic study. After all, just look at the tremendous effort that goes into attempts to break the habit. Look at the energy fueling all those attempts to repair the damage done—the turns to counseling, the therapists, priests, pastors, and others working in these awful trenches to help the addicted get their real lives back. Look at the technological ingenuity too—the new software, the filters, the countercultural and uphill efforts here and there to thwart pornography's public crawl.

To survey that multifaceted record of struggle, fledgling but growing by the day, against the also growing empirical record of the beast's harms, is to grasp a truth about the postrevolutionary male paradox that lies beyond the ridicule of the jaded or the vituperative recriminations of those still in the pit. It is to see redemption. It is to spy hope in a place where desperate people need it most—and plenty of it, too.

4 What Is the Sexual Revolution Doing to Children?

The "Pedophilia Chic", Then and Now

One of the problems with any revolution is that the beast almost inevitably becomes too forceful to control; and such is certainly true of the revolution under inspection here. That is why, for example, those who would set a new moral line at "consenting adults" miss one of the most important facts about what really happened in the world after the Pill. Not only adults but also children were to be swept into the revolution's tide—including as possible objects of adult sexual designs. We can consider this matter via a microcosm of the Zeitgeist that was highly indicative: the unexpected furor in America in 2009 over a crime committed decades before by a famous director.

The reason that the monstrous crime of pedophilia matters is simple: In an increasingly secular age, it is one of the few taboos about which people on both sides of the religious divide can agree. It remains a marker of right and wrong in a world where other markers have been erased.

And that is also the reason that the questions surrounding the attempted extradition of Roman Polanski in 2009 for a 1977 child rape briefly became Rorschach tests of our times. Sophistication vs. prudery, the morality of the 1970s vs. the morality of today, European artistes vs. American law, Hollywood vs. Middle America: Given just how many cultural and moral buttons were punched by the case, it is small wonder that *l'affaire Polanski* generated commentary as voluminous and passionate as it did.

Even so—and to the surprise of many commentators—one singularly interesting fact about the whole wretched matter was that the director and his fate generated little sympathy anywhere in the United States east of, say, Malibu. To the contrary, the Polanski case somehow succeeded in doing what no one actually trying has managed to do in years: uniting practically all Americans, liberal as well as conservative—in this case, against the hapless director.

It's been a long time since the left in America has competed with the right for the high ground over a morals charge, but such was the weirdly intriguing scramble following Polanski's arrest in Switzerland in September 2009. One of the manifestos that helped catapult the case into a media frenzy—the bluntly titled "Reminder: Polanski Raped a Child"—appeared first in the left-leaning *Salon*, then went ricocheting around the blogosphere with the firm assent of many more socially conservative sites.[1] The *New York Times* and the *Washington Post*, also untrue to form, found themselves editorializing about the case in phrases that the *Washington Times* or the Catholic League could have reprinted verbatim. And on the unaccustomed consensus went. "If the propriety of punishing child rapists were the only issue in the country," as one conservative blogger noted at the height of cyberspace's attention to

---

[1] Kate Harding, "Reminder: Roman Polanski Raped a Child", *Salon*, September 28, 2009, http://www.salon.com/2009/09/28/polanski_arrest/.

the case, "I do believe we could hold hands with the left and sing Kumbayah."[2]

The question, of course, is *why* all this welcome unanimity? After all, it wasn't very long ago that some enlightened folk took a considerably more relaxed view of the question of sex with youngsters, and they weren't afraid to say so. From the 1970s through the 1990s, in particular, a number of trial balloons were floated that almost no one in America would dare release now. Some people, including celebrated novelists, asked outright whether sex with minors might be worth a cheer or two. Other sophisticated voices wondered aloud whether "intergenerational sex" was really as bad as all that, at least where boys were concerned. Still others staked a claim to what might be called "anti-anti-pedophilia". This was the frequently expressed notion that the sexual abuse of children, although wrong, had given rise to something that also was wrong—a kind of national hysteria, an instantiation of Richard Hofstadter's famed American "paranoid style".

Given the public record of those years, it seemed, if anything, overdue to talk of "pedophilia chic", as I did in the *Weekly Standard* in two essays written several years apart (1996 and 2001).[3] Those essays consisted mostly of quotations— sometimes long ones—from a variety of public sources. They

[2] "Leftists and Conservatives Can Agree: Polanski Is a Child Rapist Who Should Face Justice", *Patterico's Pontifications*, September 30, 2009, http://patterico.com/2009/09/30/leftists-and-conservatives-can-agree-polanski-is-a-child-rapist-who-should-face-justice/.

[3] Mary Eberstadt, "Pedophilia Chic", *Weekly Standard* 1, no. 39 (June 17, 1996): http://www.weeklystandard.com/Content/Protected/Articles/000/000/007/364gmpep.asp. "'Pedophilia Chic' Reconsidered", *Weekly Standard* 6, no. 16 (January 1, 2001): http://www.weeklystandard.com/Content/Protected/Articles/000/000/010/500geaie.asp.

demonstrated something that most people would have thought shocking then, as most people still do today—that the moral dumbing-down of both pedophilia (sexual attraction to children) and ephebophilia (sexual attraction to teenagers) was making slow but steady progress in sophisticated society. And while a few critics resisted having that record held to the light, their objections were beside the point. The facts themselves about who said what during those years to define down the phenomenon of sex with minors were beyond dispute. They still are.

The phenomenon of pedophilia chic revealed the intensely troubling possibility that society, especially literate and enlightened society, was in the process of sanctioning certain exceptions to the taboo against sex with minors— particularly sex between men and boys. As a matter of criminal law, of course, girls are often and tragically the victims of older men. But pedophilia chic concerned not the rate of criminal conviction but rather the open public questioning of the taboo itself. What the record through the 1990s showed was that in the case of girls the taboo remained solid, and in the case of boys it did not. In other words, to take the example before us now, had Roman Polanski been arrested for the same crime a decade ago, in all likelihood we would have witnessed the same outcry that we did this fall.

So now let us ask the more difficult question: Would Polanski in 2009 still have inadvertently united almost everyone in America against him if his victim had been a thirteen-year-old boy rather than a thirteen-year-old girl? The answer, perhaps surprisingly, is yes—and for interesting if unexpected reasons.

Plainly, the boundaries of public discussion, at least about the subject of sex with youngsters, are more restrictive today than they were in the 1990s. Back then, the toxic moral fallout of the 1960s and 1970s was fresher and lay more visibly in the public square. For example, the *New Republic* published a short piece called "Chickenhawk" (pedophile slang for a young boy) that discussed a short film about the North American Man–Boy Love Association.[4] The piece expressed sympathy for the pederasts and would-be pederasts depicted and echoed them in asking whether the *boys* weren't sometimes the predators in man-boy sex. The piece is so damning of itself—so perfectly representative of a time when wondering aloud about "man-boy sex" exacted no penalty from the readers of a major magazine—that one could quote almost any sentence for the desired effect: "It might even be that a budding young stud had the upper hand over the aging, overweight loner", for example.

When it came time to speak about Polanski, however, bloggers for the same magazine seemed to compete over who could most thunderously denounce the confessed child rapist and his apologists. Most important, many were not just attacking the idea of sex with *girl* minors but with all minors, period.

Similarly, seventeen years ago another sophisticated magazine, *Vanity Fair*, published a whitewashing of a Phillips Exeter Academy teacher who had been caught surreptitiously filming boys in the showers and splicing those images into pornographic movies.[5] The essay not only painted this former teacher as a victim of his accusers but also cast negatively one accuser who had come forward. Along the way, the article conflated pedophilia with homosexuality,

[4] "Chickenhawk", Washington Diarist feature, *New Republic*, May 8, 1995.
[5] Jesse Kornbluth, "Exeter's Passion Play", *Vanity Fair*, December 1992.

blaming the teacher's victimization on a school atmosphere that allegedly left him stuck "in the closet".

The notion that such an apologia could appear in *Vanity Fair* or any similar venue today is simply grotesque. To the contrary, that magazine's blog also ran over with commentators weighing in vehemently against Polanski at the height of that public furor.

Example three: In 1998 the prestigious *Psychological Bulletin*, published by the American Psychological Association (APA), printed a subsequently notorious study called "A Meta-Analytic Examination of Assumed Properties of Child Sexual Abuse Using College Samples".[6] In it, three researchers took issue with "the common belief that child sexual abuse causes intense harm, regardless of gender". The authors further criticized the use of conventional terms such as "victim" and "perpetrator" and recommended that "a willing encounter with positive reactions" be labeled "simply adult-child sex". For good measure, they also compared "consensual" adult-child sex to other behaviors that the APA once considered pathological but does no more—plainly implying that such a practice would someday become as normalized in therapeutic circles as had these predecessors.

Can anyone imagine a similar study being published in a similarly prestigious venue today? A Google search of the APA's website suggests that the last time the word "pedophilia" was even used there was in 1999—tellingly, in a letter written to Tom DeLay, attempting to distance the institution from the article: "It is the position of the Association", the letter said, "that sexual activity between children

---

[6] Bruce Rind, Philip Tromovich, and Robert Bauserman, "A Meta-Analytic Examination of Assumed Properties of Child Sexual Abuse Using College Samples", *Psychological Bulletin* 124, no. 1 (1998): 22–53.

and adults should never be considered or labeled as harmless or acceptable." [7]

Or consider one last and especially surreal example. Back in 1989, the *Nation* published a short piece called "On Truth and Fiction" by a novelist who said he had lately penned an "entertainment about a San Francisco private eye who wandered into the business of transporting Haitian boys to boy-lovers all over the world". Apparently in the interest of promoting that book, the novelist wanted to report to the *Nation*'s readers that he'd lately verified its "factual basis", thanks in part to a "charming and cultivated American priest [in Haiti] who educated boys for export". During a visit to the island, the author also enjoyed a "tour of the house of Monsieur G., who was in the business of cultivating, training, and exporting comely lads". At a party at G.'s house, one of the other guests, a Frenchman, explains why he is visiting Haiti—because "his insomnia required two black boys every evening, two different ones each night". [8]

And on the worldly story went, with yet more Scotch poured by yet more houseboys in white shorts, and "other fun ... preceding the orgy" that night (before which the author allegedly departed). In sum, "On Truth and Fiction"—which appeared at the height of the AIDS crisis, a time when Haitian boy prostitutes were dying by the boatload—was a horror. But it is also a perfect instantiation of the kind of pedophilia chic that only a few years ago raised no eyebrows whatsoever in certain enlightened places.

[7] Raymond D. Fowler, "Letter to the Honorable Rep. Delay", American Psychological Association, September 9, 1999, http://www.apa.org/releases/childsexabuse.html.

[8] Herbert Gold, "On Truth and Fiction", *Nation*, December 18, 1989, http://www.thenation.com/archive/truth-and-fiction.

Once again, that kind of nod to pederasty would be far less likely to make the pages of any magazine sold in public today. In fact, if such a piece *were* to appear, it would excite plenty of comment—including calls for international investigation and prosecution of some of the characters in the tale. As if to clinch the point, the same *Nation* magazine that published such nonchalant reportage about pedophile sex tourism more than twenty years ago also happened in 2009 to publish one of the more blistering pieces on the Polanski matter—a column by feminist Katha Pollitt that was catapulted into heavy circulation on the Internet. Hollywood's apologism for the director, she concluded, "shows the liberal cultural elite at its preening, fatuous worst. . . . No wonder Middle America hates them."[9]

So what happened to turn yesterday's "intergenerational sex" into today's bipartisan demands to hang Roman Polanski and related offenders high? Mainly, I would argue, what happened was something unexpected and momentous: the Catholic priest scandals of the early years of this decade, which for two reasons have profoundly changed the ground rules of what can—and cannot—be said in public about the seduction and rape of the young.

First, the scandals made clear that one point was no longer in dispute: The sexual abuse of the young leaves real and lasting scars. In the years before the scandals, as the foregoing examples and many others show, a number of writers contested exactly that. Today, however—thanks to a great many victims testifying otherwise in the course of the priest scandals—it is hard to imagine them daring to do the same.

[9] Katha Pollitt, "Roman Polanski Has a Lot of Friends", *Nation*, October 1, 2009, http://www.thenation.com/blog/roman-polanski-has-lot-friends.

All those grown men breaking down on camera as they looked back on their childhoods, describing in heartrending testimony what it meant to be robbed of their innocence—it will take a long time to wipe such powerful images from the public mind again. At least for now, no one would dare declare that the victims had gotten what was coming to them, or that they had somehow asked for it, or that seduction by an adult was not as bad as all that— three notions that were most definitely making the rounds before the scandals broke. Moreover, that the vast majority of victims were male—81 percent, according to the definitive study by the John Jay College of Criminal Justice— proved a particularly potent antidote to the poison about boys that had been circulating earlier.[10]

In a fascinating bit of moral jujitsu, the scandals helped in a second way to repair the preexisting public consensus against sex with minors. Naturally enough, throughout the scandals and beyond, the spectacle of priests committing crimes proved irresistible to the people who already hate the Catholic Church. Also attracted by the fray were other, more refined souls who simply wish the Church ill as a matter of habit because they want it to conform more to what they mean by "Catholic". And so, throughout the scandals, the subsets of Church detractors—non-Catholics, anti-Catholics, and anti-Church-hierarchy Catholics—took every opportunity to excoriate the institution and claim the moral high ground for themselves.

---

[10] *The Nature and Scope of the Problem of Sexual Abuse of Minors by Catholic Priests and Deacons in the United States: A Research Study Conducted by the John Jay College of Criminal Justice*, published by the John Jay College of Criminal Justice and available online at www.jjay.cuny.edu/churchstudy/main/asp, Executive Summary, xi.

There was plenty of high ground for them to claim. Some Church officials stupidly played ostrich about the scandals. Others formally or informally cooperated in the evil of the crimes. With so much blame to go around, critics from all directions could hardly be faulted for turning the scandals into an opportunity to air every other grievance they harbored about Christianity—most especially, about its traditional teachings on sexual morality.

Yet this hate-fest on the Catholic Church in the name of the priest-boy scandals, rollicking though it was for some, came with blowback: It prospectively cast all those enlightened people into a new role as defenders of the young and innocent. In other words, it logically created a whole new class of antipederasts. And since the Church's harshest critics are, generally speaking, the same sort of enlightened folks from whom pedophilia chic had floated up, there lurked in all of this a contradiction. After all, one could either point to the grave moral wrong of what the offending priests had done—*or* one could minimize the suffering of the victims, as apologists for pedophilia had been doing before the scandals broke. But one could not plausibly do both any more, at least not in public. And so, in a way that could not have been predicted, but that is obviously all to the good, the priest scandals made it impossible to take that kinder, gentler look at the question of sex with youngsters that some salonistes of a few years back had been venturing.

Look, for a contrast, at Europe. Why, following Polanski's arrest, did some among the continent's elite—along with Europeanized Americans, like many in Hollywood—take a blasé view of child rape? The most obvious answer remains: the priest scandals, which America suffered in far greater numbers than did Europe. The scandals operated here as a lustration not only of the Church and her seminaries but also of public opinion—including the public declarations of the most secular of commentators.

Before cheering for this unexpected and welcome new order, we should bear in mind certain other truths. First, to say that the double standard concerning sexual exploitation of the young has eroded markedly is not to say that it has disappeared altogether.

Most serious, globalization appears to be making sex crimes against the young ever easier. Consider the exposure in France in 2009 of Fréderic Mitterand—the minister of culture who was one of Polanski's leading defenders—as a sex tourist whose autobiographical novel speaks frankly of his use of boy prostitutes in Thailand. ("I got in the habit of paying for boys", he explained.)[11] Along with those who do not believe sex with minors is all that bad, there are others who are actively pursuing children, whether in person or in cyberspace.

Third, there remain prominent salons where pedophilia has not lost its chic. Witness the *louche* reaction to the Polanski case emanating from most of Hollywood. It was as if someone had brought to life novelist Bruce Wagner's ferociously depressing 1996 novel *I'm Losing You*, a horrifying but largely believable depiction of Hollywood decadence including child molestation.[12] As Jonah Goldberg noted, the apologism for Polanski has been interesting in its own right as "a dye marker, 'lighting up' a whole archipelago of morally wretched people".[13]

---

[11] Katrin Bennhold, "French Culture Minister Refuses to Resign over Paid Sex Trysts", *New York Times*, October 8, 2009, p. A6.

[12] Bruce Wagner, *I'm Losing You* (New York: Villard, 1996).

[13] Jonah Goldberg, "Polanski Controversy Shouldn't Be Controversial", syndicated column, *National Review Online*, October 2, 2009, http://www.nationalreview.com/articles/228335/polanski-controversy-shouldnt-be-controversial/jonah-goldberg.

Even so, let's welcome the good news whenever we can get it. The public furor in America over Roman Polanski's rape of a thirteen-year-old girl many years ago revealed forcefully that in most of the country, yesterday's itinerant savoir-faire about sex with minors has been pushed from the mainstream and forced back underground. It is a consensus that did not exist in such force a decade ago, and the priest scandals are largely responsible for it.

If there's a clearer case of good coming out of evil lately, it will take some time to think of one. Meanwhile we can be thankful, at least for now, for something that so often eludes the world—a case of small but real moral progress that bodes a little better for the youngest and most innocent among us, even as it confirms that the sexual revolution has made the world a more dangerous place for them.

5 What Is the Sexual Revolution Doing to Young Adults?

What to Do about Toxic U?

Cynics will say it was ever thus, and this time the cynics will be wrong. There are indeed some new things under the sun or—perhaps more accurately, given the nocturnal nature of the beast—under the moon in higher education these days.

Welcome to the halls of "Toxic U", a school of experiential learning to which parents are never invited. Toxic U is not always visible; many students aren't even aware of it day to day. It exists in a kind of shadow world, entered itinerantly from one's dorm room through something like a looking glass—or, more likely, through that first accepted Facebook invitation to what turns out to be the wildest party on a given Saturday night. Often, that's how the newbies matriculate.

Every autumn, as regularly as bells chime in campus clock towers, some unknown number of the fresh and the young and the promising slip through that modern-looking glass onto a different quad. It features things that many have never known before and from which no one in authority can protect them now. At Toxic U there are no authorities; instead, there are predators and prey. By day, its students look like everyone else on their campuses—talented, hopeful, and privileged beneficiaries of the finest universities and colleges in the world. By night, on that other quad, some would be as unrecognizable as werewolves to the people with whom they have hitherto spent their lives.

With the exception of a glimpse via Tom Wolfe's brilliant, underrated 2004 novel, *I Am Charlotte Simmons*—which paints, in extraordinary detail, the step-by-step descent into just such a world of a naive young girl on scholarship and in search of social status at a prestigious school—this is barely charted terrain.[1] Once in a while, one or another relevant new study pops up, such as the 2007 *Campus Sexual Assault (CSA) Study*, reporting that an eye-opening 19 percent of college women said they had experienced "completed or attempted sexual assault since entering college", or any number of other studies showing that binge drinking and heavy alcohol use are higher among college students, male and female, than in the noncollege population.[2]

More often, other such studies do not make the headlines they should. One 2004 study in the *American Journal of Preventive Medicine*, for example, shows that either having sex or taking drugs or both significantly raises the risk for suicide and depression in young people and that adolescents who do not have sex or do drugs are at low risk for

---

[1] Tom Wolfe, *I Am Charlotte Simmons: A Novel* (New York: Farrar, Straus and Giroux, 2004).

[2] Christopher P. Krebs et al., *The Campus Sexual Assault (CSA) Study*, research report submitted to the National Institute of Justice, October 2007, section 5, p. 3, which emphasizes that "women at universities are at considerable risk for experiencing sexual assault, especially AOD [alcohol or drug]-related sexual assault." Numerous studies have also shown that college students drink more and more often than their peers in the noncollege population. See, for example, Grace M. Barnes et al., "Comparisons of Gambling and Alcohol Use among College Students and Noncollege Young People in the United States", *Journal of American College Health* 58 (2010): 443–52.

suicide and depression.[3] Such glimpses behind the facade of Toxic U quickly pass, however. Soon enough, no one's looking, and the traffic back and forth from the day campus to the nocturnal one goes on as usual.

It's not as if parents do not have reasons—sometimes hundreds of thousands of reasons—to look the other way. *Everybody's a little wild in college*, we all tell ourselves; *it's part of growing up. Besides, who am I to talk? And, anyway, my Jennifer or Jason is no one to worry about.* Clinging to one such consoling monologue or another, many parents will know little or nothing of their children's extracurricular life after that tearful goodbye in late August at the hugging tree.

Of course many mothers and fathers—fortunate souls—will not have to worry about Toxic U at all. Similarly, many students will thrive in their four years on campus—and how could they not? American colleges and universities, at their best, remain among the most glorious and thrilling places on earth. Plenty of young men and women will graduate exactly as was promised—as the beneficiaries of expanded intellectual, social, and other horizons, replete with fond memories and enriched understanding—and with dignity and sense of self remaining intact.

This chapter is not about those students. It is, instead, about those who, like Charlotte Simmons, arrive naive to Toxic U, have experiences antithetical to those of the students who thrive, and exit four years later exploited and changed for the worse. *I Am Charlotte Simmons* is fiction at its best—meaning that the existence of real people like Charlotte has become an increasingly well-documented fact that is one more legacy of the sexual revolution.

[3] Denise D. Hallfors et al., "Adolescent Depression and Suicide Risk: Association with Sex and Drug Behavior", *American Journal of Preventive Medicine* 27, no. 3 (2004): 224–31.

Begin with one of Toxic U's defining pastimes: binge drink-ing. College students today drink far more heavily than most of their parents will remember—or believe. A 2007 report from the U.S. Surgeon General notes that around 80 percent of students drink alcohol; no surprise there.[4] But 40 percent of students report binge drinking, defined by the Centers for Disease Control as at least five or more drinks in under two hours for men and four or more for women.[5] And remem-ber: Those numbers are just the *minimum* definitions of binge drinking. Furthermore, one in five students engages in "fre-quent episodic heavy consumption", which is defined as hav-ing binged three or more times over the preceding two weeks.

As drinking increases on campus—no surprise here, either—so do fatalities. According to a 2009 article in the *Journal of Studies on Alcohol and Drugs*, "Alcohol-related deaths among college students ages 18–24 rose from 1,440 in 1998 to 1,825 in 2005", the last year for which the researchers had data.[6] The problem appears particularly likely to penal-ize young women, who usually are smaller than men and who metabolize alcohol differently from men. Hence, as most adults know but many students apparently do not, women get drunker than men from the same amount of alcohol—a point to which we will return.

To anyone still doubting that the binge drinking scene at Toxic U really is different, at least in quantity, than most of

<hr/>

[4] *The Surgeon General's Call to Action to Prevent and Reduce Underage Drink-ing* (Washington, D.C.: U.S. Department of Health and Human Services, 2007), p. 12.

[5] Ibid., footnote 5, p. 12.

[6] Ralph W. Hingson, Wenxing Zha, and Elissa R. Weitzman, "Magnitude of and Trends in Alcohol-Related Mortality and Morbidity among U.S. Col-lege Students Ages 18–24, 1998–2005", *Journal of Studies on Alcohol and Drugs*, Supplement no. 16 (2009), http://www.ncbi.nlm.nih.gov/pmc/articles/PMC2701090/.

what came before, consider a quick tour of the campus linguistic scene. Like arrow loops in medieval castles, the slang called into being by binge drinking offers slivers of windows on a world otherwise unseen.

"Pre-gaming", for instance, refers to drinking fairly large amounts (usually belts of hard liquor) on the early side of an evening, before going out. "Shotcicles"—a highly efficient innovation likely untried by Boomer parents—are vodka-infused ice cubes, both potent and easy to hide. The terms "beer slut" and "beer whore" are likely self-explanatory; they also reflect the continuing reality that girls are not exactly treated with kid gloves at Toxic U, especially by boys with, say, a six-pack and half a fifth of vodka inside. To be wearing "beer goggles" means to have had so much to drink that one finds available members of the opposite sex more attractive than one would if one weren't so drunk. (Example: "When I saw that dog the next day, I knew I must have had my beer goggles on when I picked her up.") And a "safety buzz"—an innovative term of almost metaphysical charm—refers to the state of having ingested just enough of some mind-altering substance to be able to claim deniability or reduced culpability for what happened afterward.

Something else new under the moon at Toxic U—and well documented of late—is the change in what might laughably be called romantic mores. What most parents knew as "dating" has been replaced at Toxic U by what many of their sons and daughters know as the hookup culture. This culture is defined, primarily, as involving one or another kind of sex act at any given time between people who may or may not know each other, with the understood proviso that the act leaves no strings attached. No, the hookup culture does not describe what all the college students of the land are up to every night of the week. But for certain students—those in the habit of slipping, here or there, into Toxic U—it is one more part of a world that their parents almost certainly would not recognize.

In 2006, a particularly informative (if also exquisitely depressing) contribution to understanding hookups was made by *Unprotected: A Campus Psychiatrist Reveals How Political Correctness in Her Profession Endangers Every Student*, a book first published anonymously.[7] The author was subsequently revealed to be Miriam Grossman, a psychiatrist who treated more than two thousand students at UCLA and who grew alarmed by what she saw. In her book she cites numbers suggesting that psychiatric-consultation hours doubled in a few years and notes that 90 percent of campus counseling centers nationwide reported an upsurge in students with serious psychiatric problems.

She also describes some of her own mental-health cases and their common denominators: drinking to oblivion, drugging, one-night sex, sexually transmitted diseases, and all the rest of the hookup-culture trappings. In 2007, as if to confirm the point, *Washington Post* journalist Laura Sessions Stepp published the widely discussed *Unhooked: How Young Women Pursue Sex, Delay Love, and Lose at Both*.[8] Stepp's book was based on interviews with many high-school and college girls. In it, the author argued that hooking up actually had become the "primary" sexual interaction of the young.

[7] Miriam Grossman, *Unprotected: A Campus Psychiatrist Reveals How Political Correctness in Her Profession Endangers Every Student* (New York: Sentinel Trade, 2007).

[8] Laura Sessions Stepp, *Unhooked: How Young Women Pursue Sex, Delay Love, and Lose at Both* (New York: Riverhead Books, 2007).

One more particularly insightful look at the intersection of the bingeing and hookup cultures is Koren Zailckas' book *Smashed: Story of a Drunken Girlhood* (2006), in which she details her activities at Syracuse University and elsewhere.[9] As that and several other confessional accounts go to show, skeptics who say it was ever thus miss the boat. It isn't only that dating has turned, for some, into no-strings hookups. It isn't only that drinking, or even heavy drinking, has turned, for certain others, into drinking to oblivion. It is at the intersection of those two trends that one finds the core curriculum of Toxic U.

The link between binge drinking and the likelihood of sexual aggression for both men and women is clear. For example, the authors of a 1993 book, *Sexual Assault on Campus: The Problem and the Solution*, used figures from the studies then available to estimate that in cases that fell under the rubric of "acquaintance rape", some three-quarters of the men and half of the women were drinking at the time of the assault.[10] Such figures track with more recent ones. The 2007 *Campus Sexual Assault (CSA) Study* mentioned earlier was prepared for the Department of Justice and was based on surveys of more than 6,800 students. It likewise noted several substance-related traits that significantly raised the risk for assault. Among these were how often the women reported getting drunk, how often they had sex when drunk, and how often they attended fraternity parties. The *CSA* report also specifies that freshman and sophomore girls are at far greater risk than are older

[9] Koren Zailckas, *Smashed: Story of a Drunken Girlhood* (New York: Penguin, 2006).

[10] Carol Bohmer and Andrea Parrot, *Sexual Assault on Campus: The Problem and the Solution* (New York: Lexington Books, 1993), p. 198.

students—a fact that is not widely known and likely to be of keen interest to those with daughters in their first or second year of college.[11]

Fraternity membership also pops up in a meaningful way in these studies—another fact that does not see the light of day nearly as often as it should. More than a quarter of the women who reported cases of "incapacitated sexual assault", for example—that is, women who admitted to having been too drunk or stoned or date-drugged to give "meaningful consent"—also reported that a fraternity member was the assailant. (According to various other sources, by the way, many college men are unaware that sex acts without "meaningful consent" are, by definition, illegal.) Similarly, just being a sorority member also significantly raises the risk of sexual assault, both because sorority members, as a group, drink more than other young women on campus and because they associate more frequently with men from fraternities. Many people, including parents, rationalize away the frat-boy problem with the notion that boys will be boys. If the data are right, they are in the wrong.

One more confirmation of the connection between binge drinking and sexual aggression comes from the intriguing work of Thomas Johnson, a psychologist at Indiana State University. Johnson has studied drinking games by polling hundreds of students about their reasons for engaging in them. He found that 44 percent of the men—an intriguingly high percentage—reported "sexual manipulation" as their motivation for playing. Another impressive percentage of the men—20 percent—said they had done things after playing drinking games that would qualify as sexual assault. These games, too, are disproportionately to be found

[11] Krebs et al., *Campus Sexual Assault (CSA) Study*, p. xiv.

in the Greek system—a fact that does not mean all fraternity brothers are also pledges at Toxic U, but does mean that Greek life obviously is sending a reliable supply of recruits there.

One final feature that separates students attending Toxic U from those who have gone before is the unprecedented public attention that public sexual displays garner on some quads. Much of this public display is orchestrated by students themselves, to little apparent controversy. Certain academic departments, for example, include courses in which pornography is "studied" as an art form or for its purported social meaning. There is extracurricular stuff too, including pornographic movies shown at parties attended by girls as well as boys—another illustration of how times have changed even since the notorious sixties. Sometimes, in the name of the First Amendment, more ambitious projects flower. In 2009, for example, several campuses across the country screened *Pirates II*, which was billed as the most expensive pornographic film ever made. When the University of Maryland refused to do so because of political pressure from a congressman, student outrage was one visible result.[12]

Then there's the apparently booming business of "Sex Week". Founded by a Yale student in 2002, the event—which has since spread to many other campuses—is an extended experiment in ideological doublespeak. Sex Week purports piously to "push students to think about sex, love, intimacy, and relationships in ways they never have before". To translate, the event brings professional sadists and masochists, pornographic movie stars, and other

---

[12] Laura Fitzpatrick, "Pirates XXX: One University's Battle over Porn", *Time*, April 8, 2009.

commercial specialists in sexual esoterica to campus to instruct students in history about how to have sex.[13]

Those who defend Sex Week and its like with pious appeals to free speech seem never to have considered just who benefits most from pushing more "sexual awareness" onto the most sexualized generation yet to walk the earth. One of Sex Week's sponsors is a company that describes itself, primly, as "the nation's fastest growing in-home direct sales company specializing in romance and relationship enhancement products". In addition to spreading its wares all over campus during Sex Week, the company also stands to benefit financially in yet one more way, and from its access to young women in particular. Apparently patterning its sales method on the Avon and Tupperware models of in-home sales, it invites women over eighteen to join the ranks of its purported forty thousand consultants and to hawk products to their neighbors and friends. American Apparel is also a sponsor of Sex Week, a fact the company mentions as it pitches its underwear to college girls.

The good news is that the bad news about Toxic U has at least gotten serious, well-meaning people to consider how to improve matters.

The binge-drinking epidemic has led many colleges to tighten their rules. At Cornell University, to take one of numerous examples, administrators have been working to reform the system. The university no longer allows freshmen to attend Greek parties where alcohol is served, for

---

[13] For a detailed report, see Nathan Harden, "Bawd and Man at Yale", *National Review Online*, March 25, 2010, http://www.nationalreview.com/articles/229398/bawd-and-man-yale/nathan-harden.

example. (Such parties currently are part of the recruiting process, as they are at fraternities and sororities everywhere.) Similarly, since the headline murder of a young woman by her estranged boyfriend, both lacrosse players, at the University of Virginia in May 2010, UVA has been looking for new ways to flag potentially dangerous students. One thing the school has done, for example, is to establish a rule that any student involved in an encounter with the police has to report that fact to campus authorities or stand in violation of the honor code.

One interesting—albeit, perhaps, counterintuitive—effort to detoxify the American college campus began in 2008 under the auspices of the Amethyst Initiative. Started by a group of current and former university and college presidents and chancellors frustrated by present levels of alcohol-driven deaths and related tragedies, the Amethyst Initiative argues that the federal law maintaining the drinking age at twenty-one—a law in place since 1984—is not only an enforcement failure but also indirectly responsible for the "culture of dangerous, clandestine binge drinking" itself. Allow students to drink more openly and legally, the argument runs, and "pre-gaming" and the rest of the furtive and fast imbibing of hard spirits will become less attractive.

It is an argument that resonates with many adults who went to college when the drinking age was eighteen and whose experience of drinking alcohol consisted, say, of going out for pizza and beer rather than blacking out and getting their stomachs pumped. For what it is worth, in the course of researching Toxic U, I also asked a number of current college students of my acquaintance, scattered on campuses across the country, what they think the solution to binge drinking might be. One said spiritual renewal. The rest said the same thing as the Amethyst Initiative: Lower the drinking age.

The problem with this otherwise congenial argument can be summarized in two words, however: cars and boys. Data on traffic fatalities since 1984 confirm that death rates went down when the drinking age went up. And although the causal connection may not be quite as ironclad as most people assume—some researchers question whether enforcing seat-belt laws might have done the trick instead—almost everyone finds it intuitively obvious that keeping at least some alcohol out of the bloodstreams of at least some young men has made it harder for at least some of those young men to kill someone with a car. Faced with the imposing monolith of safety groups led by Mothers Against Drunk Driving (MADD), which was and remains a relentless scourge of the Amethyst Initiative, the 135 presidents and chancellors who believe otherwise seem stuck at a stalemate.

What else, then, to do about Toxic U? One possible answer: *Opt out.* Cynics, of course, will say once more that Toxic U can be accessed at any school, regardless of that school's creed—that bingeing and date rape are distributed evenly all over. But, here again, the cynics are wrong, and obviously so. To take just one uncontroversial example, binge drinking is significantly lower in California schools than in schools in the Northeast. Many other differences can be measured via crime statistics and related information about given campuses. As for the benefits of attending some religious schools, especially, the most compelling testimony often comes not from administrators or statistics monkeys but rather from students themselves.

After a nationally publicized 2010 student murder at the University of Virginia, a senior at Patrick Henry College, a conservative Christian school, penned a brief reflection on the differences between certain campuses. The past four years, he observed, had seen no murders or violent crimes at Patrick Henry. He concluded:

> Critics mock us for our strict rules like no dancing or drinking on campus, no members of the opposite sex permitted in your dorm room, nightly curfew hours—and the lack of a social atmosphere it creates. We have been the subject of books (*God's Harvard*), television shows, op-eds, and countless blogs who rant against our brand of overbearing rightwing Christianity that poisons society's freedom. Yet, what is the cost of students being able to "express" themselves? Is that freedom worth the cost of drunk driving deaths, drug related violence, and love affairs turned fatal?[14]

In September 2008, reflecting in the *Wall Street Journal* upon the differences between her own experience at supersecular Tufts University and her sister's at Michigan's Christian Hillsdale College, journalist Ashley Samelson (now McGuire) made similar observations:

> The posters on the walls in my all-female freshman dorm at Tufts offered information about eating disorders, what to do if you think you have been sexually assaulted, and suicide and depression hotlines. The Hillsdale walls that I saw were covered with advertisements for quilting clubs, charity opportunities and a listing of local churches.[15]

Despite such testimonies, there remain other and, often, compelling reasons why religious schools do not fit the bill

[14] Christopher Beach, "Tragedy on College Campuses", Family Research Council (blog), May 4, 2010, http://www.frcblog.com/2010/05/tragedy-on-college-campuses/.

[15] Ashley Samelson, "Lipstick Jungle", *Wall Street Journal*, September 26, 2008, W11.

for many. One reason is that some families aren't religious themselves or are too divided to find the option attractive. Another, doubtless more influential, reason is that most parents share a goal of sending their high-school senior to the best and most prestigious school they can—because they trust their child, rightly or wrongly, to stay out of Toxic U; because their child has academic or athletic gifts that are better served at some schools than others; because statistics show their child will get a better job coming out of a prestigious college; or because, like Tom Wolfe's Charlotte Simmons, their son or daughter wins a scholarship. What can those people do?

This brings us to a second approach: *Support the counterculture.* Here, too, and partly, if perversely, thanks to Toxic U itself, good news abounds. During the past several decades what were isolated malignancies in the sixties metastasized into today's binge and hookup cultures. Yet, by now, these same decades also have seen the raising up and radicalizing in reverse of a number of institutions and people—a small but growing counterculture—that would not have come into existence except in reaction to Toxic U.

These countercultural institutions include the nondenominational Love and Fidelity Network, which had its start at Princeton University and now has representatives on numerous other campuses. There is also the Christian Union, formed with nothing less than a mission to "reclaim the campus for Christ", and the Fellowship of Catholic University Students (FOCUS), where growth has been particularly dramatic. Founded in 1998 explicitly to resist the combined heft of "binge drinking, sexual promiscuity, and moral relativism" on campuses, in a dozen years FOCUS has expanded to more than fifty colleges and universities and more than four thousand students.

One more way to push back against Toxic U: *Bring back early marriage.* The most compelling reason for the existence of the hookup culture is not a change in human nature. It is not even a caving in to peer pressure. It is, rather (and perversely), efficiency. Students who do not expect to marry anyone they meet in college have no reason to "invest" in their romantic partners. This is one reason why yesteryear's boyfriend has become this year's one-night stand. What's needed is to change this "efficiency" expectation according to which young people will not "get serious" about anyone else until years later. The fact that this efficiency explanation comes at least as much from tuition-paying parents as from students themselves makes this recommendation an especially challenging one for mothers and fathers.

As Tom Wolfe so presciently understood, the biggest story on many campuses today is one that goes beyond the binge and hookup cultures alone. Similarly does it transcend policy quarrels over the drinking age, or scholastic ruminations about what, exactly, constitutes sexual aggression when neither party even remembers what day of the week it is.

In the end, a tour of Toxic U reveals something more profound. We have, on its grounds, in our time, the best petri dish we could want for observing what happens to young men and women when they play by the sexual revolution's rules. And the evidence in this petri dish testifies to one overriding and widely overlooked truth: Contrary to the liberation it has promised (and still promises), the revolution instead empowers the strong and penalizes the weak. Again, cynics will say that there is nothing new here, and they will be wrong—as the recent social science brought to bear goes to show. Yet the revolution continues to reach into dorm rooms with the false messages that women and men want the same sexual things and stand at the same sexual starting line. Those lies are what make the world of Toxic U go round.

This is what all the latest social science about nocturnal doings on the quad really shows us. As strong as they are, as educated as they have become, as successful in the work-force as they obviously are and will continue to be, young women nevertheless are also the bearers of a nature that is being ignored at great peril—to *them*. They are weaker con-stitutionally in the sense that the very behaviors that define Toxic U—binge drinking and hooking up—are docu-mented and said by all, including remorseful girls them-selves, to be more likely to damage girls than to damage boys.

The kids are all right, we keep being assured. *The kids are all right*. And a great many of them really are. But Charlotte Simmons wasn't all right, and, given the latest round of updates about Toxic U, we now know that she's far from alone. The question of what to do about that continues to stalk all those readers who would have saved Charlotte Sim-mons if they could.

6 The Transvaluation of Values, Part One

Is Food the New Sex?

As we have seen so far, the sexual revolution has profoundly affected the most fundamental aspects of human
relationships, including the way women view and treat men;
the way men view and treat women; and it has even undermined one of the deepest shared tasks of men and women,
which is the protection of children from forces that would
harm them. These are what might be called the empirical
legacy of the revolution's impact on the ground. No less
powerful, however, has been its legacy in the more rarified
realms of mores and ideas.

Consider, for example, this fact: Of all the truly seismic
shifts transforming daily life today—deeper than our financial fissures, wider even than our political and cultural
divides—one of the most important is also among the least
remarked. That is the chasm in attitude that separates almost
all of us now living in the Western world from almost all of
our ancestors over two things without which mankind cannot exist: food and sex.

The desire for food and the desire for sex share a number of interesting similarities, as philosophers and artists from
Aristotle onward have had occasion to remark here and there
across the centuries. But perhaps the most important link
is this: Both appetites, if pursued without regard to

consequence, can prove ruinous not only to oneself, but also to other people, and even to society itself. For that reason, both appetites have historically been subject in all civilizations to rules both formal and informal.

Thus the potentially destructive forces of sex—disease, disorder, sexual aggression, sexual jealousy, and what used to be called "home-wrecking"—have been ameliorated in every recorded society by legal, social, and religious conventions, primarily stigma and punishment. Similarly, all societies have developed rules and rituals governing food in part to avoid the destructiveness of free-for-alls over scarce necessities. And while food rules may not always have been as stringent as sex rules, they have nevertheless been stringent as needed. Such is the meaning, for example, of being hanged for stealing a loaf of bread in the marketplace, or keel-hauled for plundering rations on a ship.

These disciplines imposed historically on access to food and sex now raise a question that has not been asked before, probably because it was not even possible to imagine it until the lifetimes of the people reading this: What happens when, for the first time in history—at least in theory, and at least in the advanced nations—adults are more or less free to have all the sex and food they want?

This question opens the door to one more paradox attributable to the sexual revolution. For given how closely connected the two appetites appear to be, it would be natural to expect that people would do the same kinds of things with both appetites—that they would pursue both with equal ardor when finally allowed to do so, for example, or with equal abandon for consequence, or conversely, with similar degrees of discipline in the consumption of each.

In fact, though, evidence from the advanced West suggests that nearly the opposite seems to be true. The answer appears to be that when many people are faced with these possibilities for the very first time, they end up doing very different things—things we might signal by shorthand as mindful eating, and mindless sex. This chapter is both an exploration of that curious dynamic, and a speculation about what is driving it.

The dramatic expansion in access to food on the one hand and to sex on the other are complicated stories; but in each case, technology has written most of it.

Up until just about now, for example, the prime brakes on sex outside of marriage have been several: fear of pregnancy, fear of social stigma and punishment, and fear of disease. The Pill and its cousins have substantially undermined the first two strictures, at least in theory, while modern medicine has largely erased the third. Even HIV/AIDS, only a decade ago a stunning exception to the brand new rule that one could apparently have any kind of sex at all without serious consequence, is now regarded as a "manageable" disease in the affluent West, even as it continues to kill millions of less fortunate patients elsewhere.

As for food, here too one technological revolution after another explains the extraordinary change in its availability: pesticides, mechanized farming, economical transportation, genetic manipulation of food stocks, and other advances. As a result, almost everyone in the Western world is now able to buy sustenance of all kinds, for very little money, and in quantities unimaginable until the lifetimes of the people reading this.

One result of this change in food fortune, of course, is the unprecedented "disease of civilization" known as obesity, with its corollary ills. Nevertheless, the commonplace fact of obesity in today's West itself testifies to the point that access to food has expanded exponentially for just about everyone—so does the statistical fact that obesity is most prevalent in the lowest social classes and least exhibited in the highest.

And just as technology has made sex and food more accessible for a great many people, important extratechnological influences on both pursuits—particularly longstanding religious strictures—have meanwhile diminished in a way that has made both appetites even easier to indulge. The opprobrium reserved for gluttony, for example, seems to have little immediate force now, even among believers. On the rare occasions when one even sees the word, it is almost always used in a metaphorical, secular sense.

Similarly, and far more consequential, the longstanding religious prohibitions in every major creed against extramarital sex have rather famously loosed their holds over the contemporary mind. Of particular significance, perhaps, has been the movement of many Protestant denominations away from the sexual morality agreed upon by the previous millennia of Christendom. The Anglican abandonment in 1930 of the longstanding prohibition against artificial contraception is a special case in point, undermining as it subsequently did for many believers the very idea that *any* church could tell people what to do with their bodies, ever again. Whether they defended their traditional teachings or abandoned them, however, all Western Christian churches in the past century have found themselves increasingly beleaguered over issues of sex, and commensurately less influential over all but a fraction of the most traditionally minded parishioners.

Of course this waning of the traditional restraints on the pursuit of sex and food is only part of the story; any number of *non*religious forces today also act as contemporary brakes on both. In the case of food, for example, these would include factors like personal vanity, say, or health concerns, or preoccupation with the morality of what is consumed (more of this below). Similarly, to acknowledge that sex is more accessible than ever before is not to say that it is always and everywhere available. Many people who do not think they will go to hell for premarital sex or adultery, for example, find brakes on their desires for other reasons: fear of disease, fear of hurting children or other loved ones, fear of disrupting one's career, fear of financial setbacks in the form of divorce and child support, and so on.

Even men and women who *do* want all the food or sex they can get their hands on face obstacles of other kinds in their pursuit. Though many people really can afford to eat more or less around the clock, for example, home economics will still put the brakes on; it's not as if everyone can afford pheasant under glass day and night. The same is true of sex, which likewise imposes its own unwritten yet practical constraints. Older and less attractive people simply cannot command the sexual marketplace as the younger and more attractive can (which is why the promises of erasing time and age are such a booming business in a postliberation age). So, time and age still do circumscribe the pursuit of sex, even as churches and other conventional enforcers increasingly do not.

Still and all, the initial point stands: As consumers of both sex and food, today's people in the advanced societies are freer to pursue and consume both than almost all those who came before us; and our culture has evolved in interesting ways to exhibit both those trends.

To begin to see just how recent and dramatic this change is, let us imagine some broad features of the world seen

through two different sets of eyes: a thirty-year-old housewife from 1958 named Betty, and her granddaughter Jennifer, of the same age, today.

Begin with a tour of Betty's kitchen. Much of what she
makes comes from jars and cans. Much of it is also heavy
on substances that many people of our time are told to
minimize—dairy products, red meat, refined sugars, and
flours—because of compelling research about nutrition that
occurred after Betty's time. Betty's freezer is filled with meat
every four months by a visiting company that specializes in
volume, and on most nights she thaws a piece of this and
accompanies it with food from one or two jars. If there is
anything "fresh" on the plate, it is likely a potato. Interestingly, and rudimentary to our contemporary eyes though it
may be, Betty's food is served with what for us would appear
to be high ceremony, i.e., at a set table with family members present.

As it happens, there is little that Betty herself, who is
adventurous by the standards of her day, will not eat; the
going slogan she learned as a child is about cleaning your
plate, and not doing so is still considered bad form. Aside
from that notion though, which is a holdover to scarcer
times, Betty is much like any other American home cook
in 1958. She likes making some things and not others, even
as she prefers eating some things to others—and there, in
personal aesthetics, does the matter end for her. It's not
that Betty lacks opinions about food; it's just that the ones
she has are limited to what she does and does not personally like to make and eat.

Now imagine one possible counterpart to Betty today,
her thirty-year-old granddaughter Jennifer. Jennifer has almost
no cans or jars in her cupboard. She has no children or
husband or live-in boyfriend either, which is why her kitchen

table on most nights features a laptop and goes unset. Yet interestingly enough, despite the lack of ceremony at the table, Jennifer pays far more attention to food, and feels far more strongly in her convictions about it, than anyone she knows from Betty's time.

Wavering in and out of vegetarianism, Jennifer is adamantly opposed to eating red meat or endangered fish. She is also opposed to industrialized breeding, genetically enhanced fruits and vegetables, and to pesticides and other artificial agents. She tries to minimize her dairy intake, and cooks tofu as much as possible. She also buys "organic" in the belief that it is better both for her and for the animals raised in that way, even though the products are markedly more expensive than those from the local grocery store. Her diet is heavy in all the ways that Betty's was light: with fresh vegetables and fruits in particular. Jennifer has nothing but ice in her freezer, soymilk and various other items her grandmother would not have recognized in the refrigerator, and on the counter stands a vegetable juicer she feels she "ought" to use more.

Most important of all, however, is the difference in moral attitude separating Betty and Jennifer on the matter of food. Jennifer feels that there is a *right* and *wrong* about these options that transcend her exercise of choice as a consumer. She does not exactly condemn those who believe otherwise, but she doesn't understand why they do, either. And she certainly thinks the world would be a better place if more people evaluated their food choices as she does. She even proselytizes on occasion when she can.

In short, with regard to food, Jennifer falls within Immanuel Kant's definition of the Categorical Imperative: She acts according to a set of maxims that she wills at the same time to be universal law.

Betty, on the other hand, would be baffled by the idea of dragooning such moral abstractions into the service of food. This is partly because, as a child of her time, she was impressed—as Jennifer is not—about what happens when food is scarce (Betty's parents told her often about their memories of the Great Depression; and many of the older men of her time had vivid memories of deprivation in wartime). Even without such personal links to food scarcity, though, it makes no sense to Betty that people would feel as strongly as her granddaughter does about something as simple as deciding just what goes into one's mouth. That is because Betty feels, as Jennifer obviously does not, that opinions about food are simply de gustibus, a matter of individual taste—and only that.

This clear difference in opinion leads to an intriguing juxtaposition. Just as Betty and Jennifer have radically different approaches to food, so do they to matters of sex. For Betty, the ground rules of her time—which she both participates in and substantially agrees with—are clear: Just about every exercise of sex outside marriage is subject to social (if not always private) opprobrium. Wavering in and out of established religion herself, Betty nevertheless clearly adheres to a traditional Judeo-Christian sexual ethic. Thus, for example, Mr. Jones next door "ran off" with another woman, leaving his wife and children behind; Susie in the town nearby got pregnant and wasn't allowed back in school; Uncle Bill is rumored to have contracted gonorrhea; and so on. None of these breaches of the going sexual ethic is considered by Betty to be a good thing, let alone a celebrated thing. They are not even considered to be neutral things. In fact, they are all considered by her to be wrong.

Most important of all, Betty feels that sex, unlike food, is not de gustibus. She believes to the contrary that there is a right and wrong about these choices that transcends any individual act. She further believes that the world would be a better place, and individual people better off, if others believed as she does. She even proselytizes such on occasion when given the chance.

In short, as Jennifer does with food, Betty in the matter of sex fulfills the requirements for Kant's Categorical Imperative.

Jennifer's approach to sex is just about 180 degrees different. She too disapproves of the father next door who left his wife and children for a younger woman; she does not want to be cheated on herself, or to have those she cares about cheated on either. These ground-zero stipulations, aside, however, she is otherwise laissez-faire on just about every other aspect of nonmarital sex. She believes that living together before marriage is not only morally neutral, but actually better than not having such a "trial run". Pregnant unwed Susie in the next town doesn't elicit a thought one way or the other from her, and neither does Uncle Bill's gonorrhea, which is of course a merely private matter between him and his doctor.

Jennifer, unlike Betty, thinks that falling in love creates its own demands and generally trumps other considerations— unless perhaps children are involved (and sometimes, on a case-by-case basis, then too). A consistent thinker in this respect, she also accepts the consequences of her libertarian convictions about sex. She is pro-abortion, pro–gay marriage, indifferent to stem cell research and other technological manipulations of nature, and agnostic on the question of whether any particular parental arrangements seem best for children. She has even been known to watch pornography with her boyfriend, at his coaxing, in part to show just how very laissez-faire she is.

Most important, once again, is the difference in moral attitude between the two women on this subject of sex. Betty feels that there is a right and wrong about sexual choices that transcends any individual act, and Jennifer—exceptions noted—does not. It's not that Jennifer lacks for opinions about sex, any more than Betty does about food. It's just that, for the most part, they are limited to what she personally does and doesn't like.

Thus far, what the imaginary examples of Betty and Jennifer have established is this: Their personal moral relationships toward food and toward sex are just about perfectly reversed. Betty does care about nutrition and food, but it doesn't occur to her to extend her opinions to a moral judgment—i.e., to believe that other people *ought* to do as she does in the matter of food, and that they are wrong if they don't. In fact, she thinks such an extension would be wrong in a different way; it would be impolite, needlessly judgmental, simply not done. Jennifer, similarly, does care to some limited degree about what other people do about sex; but it seldom occurs to her to extend her opinions to a moral judgment. In fact, she thinks such an extension would be wrong in a different way in itself—because it would be impolite, needlessly judgmental, simply not done.

On the other hand, Jennifer is genuinely certain that her opinions about food are not only nutritionally correct, but also, in some deep meaningful sense, *morally* correct—i.e., she feels that others ought to do something like what she does. And Betty, on the other hand, feels exactly the same way about what she calls sexual morality.

As noted, this desire to extend their personal opinions in two different areas to an "ought" that they think should be somehow binding—binding, that is, to the idea that others should do the same—is the definition of the Kantian imperative. Once again, note: Betty's Kantian imperative concerns sex not food, and Jennifer's concerns food not sex. In just over sixty years, in other words—not for everyone, of course, but for a great many people, and for an especially large portion of sophisticated people—the moral poles of sex and food have been reversed. Betty thinks food is a matter of taste, whereas sex is governed by universal moral law of some kind; and Jennifer thinks exactly the reverse.

What has happened here?

Betty and Jennifer may be imaginary, but the decades that separate the two women have brought related changes to the lives of many millions. In the sixty years between their two kitchens, a similar polar transformation has taken root and grown not only throughout America but also throughout Western society itself. During those years, cultural artifacts and forces in the form of articles, books, movies, and ideas aimed at deregulating what is now quaintly called "nonmarital sex" have abounded and prospered; while the cultural artifacts and forces aimed at regulating or seeking to reregulate sex outside of marriage have largely declined. In the matter of food, on the other hand, exactly the reverse has happened. Increasing scrutiny over the decades to the quality of what goes into people's mouths has been accompanied by something almost wholly new under the sun: the rise of universalizable moral codes based on food choices.

Begin with the more familiar face of diets and fads—the Atkins diet, the Zone diet, the tea diet, the high-carb diet, Jenny Craig, Weight Watchers, and all the rest of the food fixes promising us new and improved versions of ourselves.

Abundant though they and all their relatives are, those short-term fads and diets are nevertheless merely epiphenomena.

Digging a little deeper, the obsession with food that they reflect resonates in many other strata of the commercial marketplace. Book reading, for example, may be on the way out, but until it goes, cookbooks and food books remain among the most reliable moneymakers in the industry. To scan the bestseller lists or page the major reviews in any given month is to find that books on food and food-thought are at least reliably represented, and sometimes even predominate—to list a few from the past few years alone: Michael Pollan's *The Omnivore's Dilemma*; Eric Schlosser's *Fast Food Nation*; Gary Taubes' *Good Calories, Bad Calories*; Bill Buford's *Heat*, and many more titles feeding the insatiable interest in food.

Then there are the voyeur and celebrity genres, which have made some chefs the equivalent of rock stars via commercial successes like *Kitchen Confidential: Adventures in the Culinary Underbelly* or *Service Included: Four-Star Secrets of an Eavesdropping Waiter* or *The Devil in the Kitchen: Sex, Pain, Madness, and the Making of a Great Chef*. Anywhere you go, anywhere you look, food in one form of consumption or another is what's on tap. The proliferation of chains like Whole Foods, the recent institution by California's governor of state-mandated nutritional breakdowns in restaurants in the state of California (a move that is likely to be repeated by governors in the other forty-nine): these and many other developments speak to the paramount place occupied by food and food choices in the modern consciousness. As the *New York Times Magazine* lately noted, in a foreword emphasizing the intended expansion of its (already sizeable) food coverage, such writing is "perhaps never a more crucial part of what we do than today—a moment when what and how we eat has emerged as a Washington issue and a global-environmental issue as well as a kitchen-table one." [1]

Underneath the passing fads and short-term fixes and notices like these, deep down where the seismic change lies, is a series of revolutions in how we now think about food—changes that focus not on today or tomorrow, but on eating as a way of life.

One recent influential figure in this tradition was George Ohsawa, a Japanese philosopher who codified what is known as macrobiotics. Popularized in the United States by his pupil Michio Kushi, macrobiotics has been the object of fierce debate for several decades now, and Kushi's book *The Macrobiotic Path to Total Health: A Complete Guide to Naturally Preventing and Relieving More Than 200 Chronic Conditions and Disorders*, remains one of the modern bibles on food. [2] Macrobiotics makes historical as well as moral claims, including the claim that its tradition stretches back to Hippocrates and includes Jesus and the Han dynasty among other enlightened beneficiaries. These claims are also reflected in the macrobiotic system, which includes the expression of gratitude (not prayers) for food, serenity in the preparation of it, and other extranutritional ritual. And even as the macrobiotic discipline has proved too ascetic for many people (and certainly for most Americans), one can see its influence at work in other serious treatments of the food question

---

[1] "A New Way to Look at Food Writing", the editors, *New York Times Magazine*, January 2, 2009, http://www.nytimes.com/2009/01/04/magazine/04FoodSeries.html?scp=1&sq=a%20new%20way%20to%20look%20at%20food%20writing&st=cse.

[2] Michio Kushi, *The Macrobiotic Path to Total Health: A Complete Guide to Naturally Preventing and Relieving More Than 200 Chronic Conditions and Disorders*, paperback edition (New York: Ballantine Books, 2004).

that have trickled outward. The current popular call to "mindful eating", for example, echoes the macrobiotic injunction to think of nothing but food and gratitude while consuming, even to the point of chewing any given mouthful at least fifty times.

Alongside macrobiotics, the past decades have also seen tremendous growth in vegetarianism and its related off-shoots, another food system that typically makes moral as well as health claims. As a movement, and depending on which part of the world one looks at, vegetarianism predates macrobiotics.[3] Vegetarian histories claim for themselves the Brahmins, Buddhists, Jainists, and Zoroastrians, as well as certain Jewish and Christian practitioners. In the modern West, Percy Bysshe Shelley was a prominent activist for the movement in the early nineteenth century; and the first Vegetarian Society was founded in England in 1847.

Around the same time in the United States, a Presbyterian minister named Sylvester Graham popularized vegetarianism in tandem with a campaign against excess of all kinds (ironically, under the circumstances, this health titan is remembered primarily for the graham cracker). Various other American religious sects have also gone in for vegetarianism, including the Seventh-Day Adventists, studies on whom make up some of the most compelling data about the possible health

---

[3] As defined by the International Vegetarian Union, a vegetarian eats no animals but may eat eggs and dairy (and is then an ovo-lacto vegetarian). A pescetarian is a vegetarian who allows the consumption of fish. A vegan excludes both animals and animal products from his diet, including honey. Vegetarians and vegans can be further refined into numerous other categories—fruitarian, Halal vegetarian, and so on. The terminological complexity here only amplifies the point that food now attracts the taxonomical energies once devoted to, say, metaphysics.

benefits of a diet devoid of animal flesh.[4] Uniting numerous discrete movements under one umbrella is the International Vegetarian Union, which started just a little more than a hundred years ago, in 1908.

Despite this long history, though, it is clear that vegetarianism *apart* from its role in religious movements did not really take off as a mass movement until relatively recently. Even so, its contemporary success has been remarkable. Pushed perhaps by the synergistic public interest in macrobiotics and nutritional health, and nudged also by occasional rallying books including Peter Singer's 1975 *Animal Liberation* and Matthew Scully's *Dominion*, vegetarianism today is one of the most successful secular moral movements in the West; whereas macrobiotics for its part, though less successful as a mass movement by name, has witnessed the vindication of some of its core ideas and stands as a kind of synergistic brother in arms.[5]

To be sure, macrobiotics and vegetarianism/veganism have their doctrinal differences. Macrobiotics limits animal flesh not out of moral indignation, but for reasons of health and Eastern ideas of proper "balancing" of the forces of yin and yang. Similarly, macrobiotics also allows for moderate amounts of certain types of fish—as strict vegetarians do not. On the other hand, macrobiotics also bans a number of vegetables (among them tomatoes, potatoes, peppers, and others

---

[4] See, for example, Gary Fraser, *Diet, Life Expectancy, and Chronic Disease: Studies of Seventh-Day Adventists and Other Vegetarians* (England: Oxford University Press, 2003), which examines data from the 1989 Adventist Health Study of over thirty-four thousand subjects.

[5] See Peter Singer, *Animal Liberation* (New York: Random House, 1975), the single most influential book of the animal welfare and animal rights movements. See also Matthew Scully, *Dominion: The Power of Man, the Suffering of Animals, and the Call to Mercy* (New York: St. Martin's Press, 2002), for the single most significant appeal to animal welfare based on Christian principles.

that are said to be too "yin"), whereas vegetarianism bans none. Nonetheless, macrobiotics and vegetarianism have more in common than not, especially from the point of view of anyone eating outside either of these codes. The doctrinal differences separating one from another are about equivalent in force today to those between, say, Presbyterians and Lutherans.

And that is exactly the point. For many people, schismatic differences about food have taken the place of schismatic differences about faith. Again, the curiosity is just how recent this is. Throughout human history, practically no one devoted this much time to matters of food as *ideas* (as opposed to, say, time spent gathering it). Still less does it appear to have occurred to people that dietary schools could be untethered from a larger metaphysical and moral worldview. Observant Jews and Muslims, among others, have had strict dietary laws from their faiths' inception, but that is just it—their laws told believers what to do with food when they got it, rather than inviting them to dwell on food as a thing in itself. Like the Adventists, who speak of their vegetarianism as being "harmony with the Creator", or like the Catholics with their itinerant Lenten and other obligations, these previous dietary laws were clearly designed to enhance religion— not replace it.

Do today's influential dietary ways of life in effect replace religion? Consider that macrobiotics, vegetarianism, and veganism all make larger health claims as part of their universality—but unlike yesteryear, to repeat the point, most of them no longer do so in conjunction with organized religion. Macrobiotics, for its part, argues (with some evidence) that processed foods and too much animal flesh are toxic to the human body, whereas whole grains, vegetables, and fruits are not. The literature of vegetarianism makes a similar point, recently drawing particular attention to new research concerning the connection between the consumption of red meat and certain cancers. In both cases, however, dietary laws are not intended to be handmaidens to a higher cause, but moral causes in *themselves*.

Just as the food of today often attracts a level of metaphysical attentiveness suggestive of the sex of yesterday, so does food today seem attended by a similarly evocative—and proliferating—number of verboten signs. The opprobrium reserved for perceived "violations" of what one "ought" to do has migrated, in some cases fully, from one to the other. Many people who wouldn't be caught dead with an extra ten pounds—or eating a hamburger, or wearing real leather—tend to be laissez-faire in matters of sex. In fact, just observing the world as it is, one is tempted to say that the *more* vehement people are about the morality of their food choices, the *more* hands-off they believe the rest of the world should be about sex. When was the last time you heard or used the word "guilt"—in conjunction with actual sin as traditionally conceived, or with having eaten something verboten or not having gone to the gym?

Perhaps the most revealing example of the infusion of morality into food codes can be found in the current European passion for what the French call *terroir*—an idea that originally referred to the specific qualities conferred by geography on certain food products (notably wine) and that has now assumed a life of its own as a moral guide to buying and consuming locally. That there is no such widespread, concomitant attempt to impose a new morality on sexual pursuits in Western Europe seems something of an understatement. But as a measure of the reach of *terroir* as a moral code, consider only a sermon from Durham Cathedral in 2007. In it, the dean explained Lent as an event that "says to us, cultivate a good *terroir*, a spiritual ecology that will re-focus our passion for God, our praying, our pursuit of justice in the world, our care for our fellow human beings".[6]

There stands an emblematic example of the reversal between food and sex in our time: in which the once-universal moral code of European Christianity is being explicated for the masses by reference to the now more-universal European moral code of consumption à la *terroir*.

Moreover, this reversal between sex and food appears firmest the more passionately one clings to either pole. Thus, for instance, though much has lately been made of the "greening" of the evangelicals, no vegetarian Christian group is as nationally known as, say, People for the Ethical Treatment of Animals or any number of other vegetarian/ vegan organizations, most of which appear to be secular or antireligious, and none of which, so far as my research shows, extend their universalizable moral ambitions to the realm of sexuality. When *Skinny Bitch*—a hip guide to veganism that recently topped the bestseller lists for months—repeatedly exhorts its readers to a life that is "clean, pure, healthy", for example, it is emphatically *not* including sex in this moral vocabulary, and makes a point of saying so.[7]

C. S. Lewis once compared the two desires as follows, to make the point that something about sex had gotten

[6] The Very Reverend Michael Sadgrove, "Terroir for Lent", Durham Cathedral, February 25, 2007, http://www.durhamcathedral.co.uk/schedule/sermons/ 130.

[7] Rory Freedman and Kim Barnouin, *Skinny Bitch* (Philadelphia, Pa.: Running Press, 2005).

incommensurate in his own time: "There is nothing to be ashamed of in enjoying your food: there would be everything to be ashamed of if half the world made food the main interest of their lives and spent their time looking at pictures of food and dribbling and smacking their lips."[8] He was making a point in the genre of reductio ad absurdum.

But for the jibe to work as it once did, our shared sense of what is absurd about it must work too—and that shared sense, in an age as visually, morally, and aesthetically dominated by food as is our own, is waning fast. Consider the coining of the term "gastroporn" to describe the eerily similar styles of high-definition pornography on the one hand and stylized shots of food on the other. Actually, the term is not even that new. It dates back at least three decades, to a 1977 essay by that title in the *New York Review of Books*. In it author Alexander Cockburn observed that

> it cannot escape attention that there are curious parallels between manuals on sexual techniques and manuals on the preparation of food; the same studious emphasis on leisurely technique, the same apostrophes to the ultimate, heavenly delights. True gastro-porn heightens the excitement and also the sense of the unattainable by proffering colored photographs of various completed recipes.[9]

With such a transfer, the polar migrations of food and sex during the last half century would appear complete.

If it is true that food is the new sex, however, where does it leave sex? This brings us to the paradox already hinted

[8] C. S. Lewis, *Mere Christianity*, in *The Complete C. S. Lewis Signature Classics* (New York: HarperOne, 2004), p. 59.
[9] Alexander Cockburn, "Gastro Porn", *New York Review of Books*, December 8, 1977, http://www.nybooks/articles/1977/dec/08/gastro-porn/?page=.

at. As the consumption of food not only literally but also figuratively has become progressively more discriminate and thoughtful, at least in theory (if rather obviously not always in practice), the consumption of sex in various forms appears to have become the opposite for a great many people, i.e., progressively more indiscriminate and unthinking.

Several proofs could be offered for such a claim, beginning with any number of statistical studies. Both men and women are far less likely to be sexually inexperienced on their wedding nights now (if indeed they marry) than they were just a few decades ago. They are also more likely to be experienced in all kinds of ways, including in the use of pornography. Like the example of Jennifer, moreover, their general thoughts about sex become more laissez-faire the further down the age demographic one goes.

Consider as further proof of the dumbing down of sex the coarseness of popular entertainment, say through a popular advice column on left-leaning *Slate* magazine called "Dear Prudence" that concerns "manners and morals". "Should I destroy the erotic video my husband and I have made?" "My boyfriend's kinky fetish might doom our relationship." "My husband wants me to abort, and I don't." "How do I tell my daughter she's the result of a sexual assault?" "A friend confessed to a fling with my now-dead husband." And so on. The mindful vegetarian slogan "You are what you eat" has no counterpart in the popular culture today when it comes to sex.

This junk sex shares all the defining features of junk food. It is produced and consumed by people who do not know one another. It is disdained by those who believe they have access to more authentic experience or "healthier" options. As we saw in chapter 2, evidence is also beginning to emerge about compulsive pornography consumption—as it did slowly but surely in the case of compulsive packaged food consumption—that this laissez-faire judgment is wrong.[10]

This brings us to another similarity between junk sex and junk food: People are furtive about both, and many feel guilty about their pursuit and indulgence of each. And those who consume large amounts of both are also typically self-deceptive, too, i.e., they underestimate just how much they do it and deny its ill effects on the rest of their lives. In sum, to compare junk food to junk sex is to realize that they have become virtually interchangeable vices—even if many people who do not put "sex" in the category of vice will readily do so with food.

At this point, if not already, the impatient reader will interject that something else—something understandable and anodyne—is driving the increasing attention to food in our day, namely, the fact that we have learned much more than humans used to know about the importance of a proper diet to health and longevity. And this is surely a point borne out by the facts of the case, too. One attraction of macrobiotics, for example, is its promise to reduce the risks of cancer. The fall in cholesterol that attends a true vegan or vegetarian diet is another example. Manifestly, one reason that people today are so much more discriminating about food is that decades of recent research have taught us that diet has more potent effects than Betty and her friends

---

[10] For clinical accounts of the evidence of harm, see, for example, Ana J. Bridges, "Pornography's Effects on Interpersonal Relationships", and Jill C. Manning, "The Impact of Pornography on Women", in *The Social Costs of Pornography: A Collection of Papers*, ed. James R. Stoner Jr. and Donna M. Hughes (Princeton, N.J.: Witherspoon Institute, 2010), pp. 69–88 and 89–110, respectively. For an interesting econometric assessment of what is spent to avoid or recover from pornography addiction, see also K. Doran, "Industry Size, Measurement, and Social Costs", in ibid., pp. 185–99.

understood, and can be bad for you or good for you in ways not enumerated before.

All that is true, but then the question is this: Why aren't more people doing the same with sex?

For here we come to the most fascinating turn of all. One cannot answer the question by arguing that there is no such empirical news about indiscriminately pursued sex and how *it* can be good or bad for you; to the contrary, there is, and lots of it. After all, several decades of empirical research—which also did not exist before—have demonstrated that the sexual revolution, too, has had consequences, and that many of them have redounded to the detriment of a sexually liberationist ethic.

Married, monogamous people are more likely to be happy. They live longer.[11] These effects are particularly evident for men. Divorced men, in particular and conversely, face health risks—including heightened drug use and alcoholism—that married men do not. While assistant professors across the land make tenure arguing over the causal vectors of these findings, researchers themselves connect the obvious dots often enough. As one for the Rand Corporation hypothesized about some 140 years of demographic evidence, for example,

> The health benefits obtained by men who stay married or remarry stem from a variety of related factors, including care in times of illness, improved nutrition, and a home atmosphere that reduces stress and stress-related illnesses,

[11] This finding has appeared consistently. See, for example, Lee A. Lillard and Constantijn W. A. Panis, "Marital Status and Mortality: The Role of Health", *Demography* 33, no. 3 (1996): 313–27. See also R. M. Kaplan and R. G. Kronick, "Marital Status and Longevity in the United States Population", *Journal of Epidemiology and Community Health* 60 (August 2006): 760–65.

encourages healthy behaviors, and discourages unhealthy ones such as smoking and excessive drinking. Influences of this type tend to enhance a man's immediate health status and may often improve his chances for a longer life.[12]

As Linda J. Waite and Maggie Gallagher, among other scholars, have documented, married men earn more and save more; and married households not surprisingly trump other households in income.[13] As Kay S. Hymowitz, among other scholars, has shown, marriage confers benefits beyond the partners themselves and onto the children.[14] Sociologist W. Bradford Wilcox, one more expert, has summarized the marriage benefit this way: "[C]hildren who grow up in intact, married families are significantly more likely to graduate from high school, finish college, become gainfully employed, and enjoy a stable family life themselves, compared to their peers who grow up in nonintact families."[15] The list could go on, but it need not; the point is plain enough. Conversely and as we have also seen earlier, divorce is often a financial catastrophe for a family, particularly the women and children in it. So is illegitimacy typically a financial disaster. Children from broken homes are at risk for all kinds of behavioral, psychological, educational, and other

[12] Lee A. Lillard and Constantijn (Stan) Panis, "Health, Marriage, and Longer Life for Men", Research Brief 5018, Rand Corporation, 1998, http://www.rand.org/pubs/research_briefs/RB5018.html.

[13] Linda J. Waite and Maggie Gallagher, *The Case for Marriage: Why Married People Are Happier, Healthier, and Better Off Financially* (New York: Doubleday, 2000), p. 98.

[14] Kay S. Hymowitz, *Marriage and Caste in America: Separate and Unequal Families in a Post-Marital Age* (Lanham, Md.: Ivan R. Dee, 2006).

[15] W. Bradford Wilcox, ed., *When Marriage Disappears: The Retreat from Marriage in Middle America* (Charlottesville, Va.: University of Virginia, National Marriage Project; New York: Institute for American Values, 2010), available online at http://stateofourunions.org/2010/when-marriage-disappears.php.

problems that children from intact homes are not. Girls and boys, numerous sources including Elizabeth Marquardt and David Blankenhorn have also shown, are adversely affected by family breakup into adulthood, and have higher risks than children from intact homes of repeating the pattern of breakup themselves.[16]

This recital touches only the periphery of the empirical record now being assembled about the costs of laissez-faire sex to American society—a record made all the more interesting by the fact that it could not have been foreseen back when sexual liberationism seemed merely synonymous with the removal of some seemingly inexplicable old stigmas. Today, however, two generations of social science replete with studies, surveys, and regression analyses galore stand between the Moynihan Report and what we know now, and the overall weight of its findings is clear. The question raised by this record is not why some people changed their habits and ideas when faced with compelling new facts about food and health; it is rather why more people have not done the same about sex.

When Friedrich Nietzsche wrote longingly of the "transvaluation of all values", he meant the hoped-for restoration of sexuality to its proper place as a celebrated, morally neutral life force. He could not possibly have foreseen our world: one in which sex would indeed become "morally neutral" in the eyes of a great many people—even as food would come to replace it as source of moral authority.[17]

---

[16] See David Blankenhorn, *Fatherless America: Confronting Our Most Urgent Social Problem* (New York: Basic Books, 1995), and Elizabeth Marquardt, *Between Two Worlds: The Inner Lives of Children of Divorce* (New York: Crown Books, 2005).

[17] Interestingly, Nietzsche does appear to have foreseen the universalizability of vegetarianism, writing in the 1870s, "I believe that the vegetarians,

Nevertheless, events have proven Nietzsche wrong about his wider hope that men and women of the future would simply enjoy the benefits of free sex without any attendant seismic shifts. For there may in fact be no such thing as a destigmatization of sex, as the events outlined in this essay suggest. The rise of a recognizably Kantian, morally universalizable code concerning food—beginning with the international vegetarian movement of the last century and proceeding with increasing moral fervor into our own times via macrobiotics, veganism/vegetarianism, and European codes of *terroir*—has paralleled exactly the waning of a universally accepted sexual code in the Western world during these same years.

Who can doubt that the two trends are related? Unable or unwilling (or both) to impose rules on sex in the wake of the revolution, yet equally unwilling to dispense altogether with the moral code that has traditionally afforded large protections, modern man has apparently performed his own act of transubstantiation. He has taken longstanding morality about sex, and substituted it onto food. The all-you-can-eat buffet is now stigmatized; the sexual smorgasbord is not.

In the end, it is hard to avoid the conclusion that the rules being drawn around food receive some force from the fact that people are uncomfortable with how far the sexual revolution has gone—and not knowing what to do about

---

with their prescription to eat less and more simply, are of more use than all the new moral systems taken together.... There is no doubt that the future educators of mankind will also prescribe a stricter diet." Also interesting, Adolf Hitler—whose own vegetarianism appears to have been adopted because of Wagner's (Wagner in turn had been convinced by the sometime vegetarian Nietzsche)—reportedly remarked in 1941 that "there's one thing I can predict to eaters of meat: the world of the future will be vegetarian."

it, they turn for increasing consolation to mining morality out of what they eat.

So what does it finally mean to have a civilization puritanical about food, and licentious about sex? In this sense, Nietzsche's fabled madman came not too late, but too early—too early to have seen the empirical library that would be amassed from the mid-twenty-first century on, testifying to the problematic social, emotional, and even financial nature of exactly the solution he sought. If there is a moral to this curious transvaluation, it would seem to be that the norms society imposes on itself in pursuit of its own self-protection do not wholly disappear, but rather mutate and move on, sometimes in curious guises. Far-fetched though it seems at the moment, where mindless food is today, mindless sex—in light of the growing empirical record of its own unleashing—may yet again be tomorrow.

7   The Transvaluation of Values, Part Two

Is Pornography the New Tobacco?

Just as the codes surrounding food and sex appear to have undergone a polar migration under the atmospheric pressure of the sexual revolution, so have two other common substances regarded as vices at different times in history—and the results here, too, go society-wide throughout the West.

Begin with one more thought experiment. Imagine a substance that is relatively new in the public square, but by now so ubiquitous in your society that a great many people find its presence unremarkable. Day in and day out, your own encounters with this substance, whether direct or indirect, are legion. Your exposure is so constant that it rarely even occurs to you to wonder what life might be like without it.

In fact, so common is this substance that you take the status quo for granted, though you're aware that certain other people disagree. A noisy minority of Americans firmly opposes its consumption, and these neo-Puritans try routinely to alert the public to what they claim to be its dangers and risks. Despite this occasional resistance, however, you—like many other people of your time—continue to regard this substance with relative equanimity. You may or may not consume the thing yourself, but even if you don't, you can't much see the point of interfering with anyone else's doing it. Why bother? After all, that particular genie's out of the bottle.

The scenario sketched in those paragraphs captures two very different moments in recent American history. One is the early 1960s, exactly the moment when tobacco is ubiquitous, roundly defended by interested parties, and widely accepted as an inevitable social fact—and is about to be propelled over the cliff of respectability and down the other side by the Surgeon General's famous 1964 "Report on Smoking and Health". The resulting social turnaround, though taking decades and unfolding still, has nevertheless been nothing short of remarkable. In 1950, almost half the adult American population smoked; by 2004, just over a fifth did. Though still in common use and still legally available, cigarettes somehow went from being widely consumed and accepted throughout the Western world to nearly universally discouraged and stigmatized—all in the course of a few decades.

The other moment in time captured by the opening thought experiment is our own, except that the substance under discussion this time around is not tobacco, but rather pornography—as ubiquitous, as roundly defended by interested parties, and as widely accepted as an inevitable social fact as smoking was fifty-odd years ago. Today's prevailing social consensus about pornography is practically identical to the social consensus about tobacco in 1963, i.e., it is characterized by widespread tolerance, tinged with resignation about the notion that things could ever be otherwise.

After all, many people reason, pornography's not going to go away any time soon. Serious people, including experts, either endorse its use or deny its harms or both. Also, it is widely seen as cool, especially among younger people, and this coveted social status further reduces the already low incentive for making a public issue of it. In addition, many people also say that consumers have a "right" to pornography—possibly even a constitutional right. No wonder so many are laissez-faire about this substance. Given the social and political circumstances arrayed in its favor, what would be the point of objecting?

Such is the apparent consensus of the times, and apart from a minority of opponents it appears very nearly bulletproof—every bit as bulletproof, in fact, as the prevailing laissez-faire public view of smoking did in 1964. In fact, just substitute the word "smoking" for that of "pornography" in the paragraph above, and the result works just as well.

And that is exactly the point of our opening thought experiment. Many people today share the notion that today's unprecedented levels of pornography consumption are somehow fixed, immutable, a natural expression of (largely but not entirely male) human nature. Even people who deplore pornography seem resigned to its exponentially expanded presence in the culture. This is one genie, most people agree, that is out of the bottle for good.

But this widely held belief, however understandable, overlooks a critical and perhaps potent fact. The example of tobacco shows that one can indeed take a substance to which many people are powerfully drawn—nicotine—and sharply reduce its consumption via a successful revival of social stigma. What might this transformation imply for today's unprecedented rates of pornography consumption? Perhaps a great deal. For in one realm after another—as a habit, as an industry, as a battleground for competing ideas of the public good—Internet pornography today resembles nothing so much as tobacco, circa a half century ago. Let us begin to count the ways.

Pornography and tobacco, we can all agree, have at least this in common: Both have been on the receiving end of stern public moralism ever since their appearance in human society. During the past few decades, however, something particularly interesting has occurred. So far as public opprobrium is concerned, at least in America (and by extension, most of the rest of the West), the two substances have essentially changed places.

To get a sense of just how drastically the social consensus about each has changed, let us invoke the imaginary examples of Betty, a thirty-year-old housewife in 1958; and Jennifer, her thirty-year-old granddaughter today. Like many of her friends, and also like her husband, Barney, Betty smokes cigarettes. She does so unself-consciously and throughout the day—in the kitchen and most other rooms of the house, during her housecleaning, on the front steps, around the children, in the car, at the movies and in restaurants, even walking down the sidewalk.

It's not the sort of thing she gives much thought to, though when she does she sometimes feels conflicted. For Betty, the issue of tobacco may raise certain questions of expediency (she worries about the money she spends on it). She also wonders from time to time about its possible effect on her health, as people by 1958 are starting to talk about that too. On the other hand, despite these occasional personal misgivings, Betty does not see smoking as a moral issue in its own right. It is rather, she believes, a matter of individual taste.

Now consider Betty's view of a different substance that is as rare in her own life as cigarettes are plentiful—pornography. Compared to the generations about to follow her, she really has not seen much of it. On the other hand, neither is she as ignorant of it as the generation before her.

Playboy magazine is a few years old in 1958, for example, and the celebrities who take off their clothes in its pages make news whether Betty sees pictures of them or not. In general, though, the issue of dirty books or pictures does not worry Betty much. The Comstock Act banning the sending of obscene materials through the mails has just been upheld in a Supreme Court case called *Roth v. United States*—this fact among others means that in Betty's world, unlike our own, such materials are still relatively hard to get.

In any event, what little Betty has seen of this material has left a firm impression. She thinks that *Playboy* and all it stands for are disgusting. She is, further, a Kantian about her opinion, and extends it to a general moral rule: Pornography, or what she would call "smut", is morally wrong. She also believes that everyone should feel as she does about it, though obviously many people do not.

Now consider the very different case of thirty-year-old Jennifer today. Jennifer is vehemently opposed to smoking tobacco. The very idea of putting a foreign substance into her lungs disgusts her. She is further a Kantian about her opinion, and extends it to a general rule: Smoking is morally wrong. She also believes that everyone should feel as she does about it, though obviously many people do not.

Interestingly, it does not occur to Jennifer to hold the rest of her body to the same strict standard as her lungs. Like many other women in her generation, she is both single and sexually experienced in ways that most women of Betty's generation would not have thought possible. As part of that experience, Jennifer knows far more than Betty could have about pornography.

Jennifer's attitude toward this substance is complicated and similar in some ways to Betty's itinerant misgivings about tobacco. On the one hand, like Betty, she does not think that this particular substance—in Jennifer's case, pornography—poses any genuine moral issue. On the other, again like Betty, when she does stop to think about it she feels conflicted. From time to time, her boyfriend Jason has persuaded Jennifer into watching some together on the Internet, "as a couple". On the outside, Jennifer goes along with this gracefully enough. On the inside, though, she is not so sure she likes this stuff—more precisely, that she likes Jason liking it. One thing she is certain of, though, is that Jason knows far more about pornography than she does.

Even so, and despite her occasional misgivings, Jennifer has the standard-issue generational opinion of her time. She is not a Kantian about it. She has her own personal likes and dislikes; she assumes everyone else does too. In sum, she does not think that pornography, when made by and for consenting adults, is morally wrong. She thinks it is a matter of individual taste.

It's important to understand just how complete the social turnaround on these two substances has been. Betty would never dream of putting even a few minutes of Internet pornography as we now know it before her eyes. She would feel degraded, polluted, even sick. To the extent that she has ever even thought about it, she thinks that pornography is morally wrong, and that the people who create it are borderline evil.

Jennifer, on the other hand, may not greet pornography with quite the gusto that her boyfriend does. But she has no such passionate feelings about it as Betty would, let alone any Kantian impulse to make a sweeping moral claim about it. On the other hand, Jennifer would never dream of putting a cigarette into her mouth. She would feel degraded, polluted, even sick. She thinks that tobacco is morally wrong, and that the people who create it are borderline evil.

The imaginary examples of Betty and Jennifer demonstrate the full turn society has taken in the past fifty years with regard to these two powerfully alluring substances, tobacco and pornography. Yesterday, smoking was considered unremarkable in a moral sense, whereas pornography was widely considered disgusting and wrong—including even by people who consumed it. Today, as a general rule, just the reverse is true. Now it is pornography that is widely (though not universally) said to be value-free, whereas smoking is widely considered disgusting and wrong—including even by many smokers. What Betty and Jennifer go to show is that the public moral status of tobacco half a century ago is strikingly similar to that of pornography today.

Of course there are a number of obvious ways in which pornography and tobacco do *not* resemble one another. But it is more interesting to reflect on the ways in which they do.

Consider the matter of harm. As we saw in chapter 3, a growing empirical record verifies the damage that can be done to human relationships by pornography. It is nevertheless a record that remains fiercely disputed in some quarters—just as the question of whether smoking did cause harm was resisted by many other people, and especially by the tobacco industry, throughout much of the twentieth century. Plainly, one other reason why the issue of harm took so long to settle is that a great many people—particularly smokers and the industry that served them—had reasons of their own for resisting the empirical evidence. Because of their desire to continue consuming cigarettes, many denied or minimized tobacco's risks.

This harm-minimizing synergy between producer and consumer is one more factor suggesting that Internet pornography may stand in the same situation today as tobacco in the decades before the Surgeon General's report. That is to say, producers in the pornography industry have a vested interest in denying that their product causes harm, and they are aided in this effort, however unwittingly, by consumers who have reasons of their own for wanting this to be true.

On the flip side of the consumer coin, the denial that the product in question causes harm is also nearly identical. A spokesman for the British Libertarian Alliance, for example, argues on behalf of pornography consumption thus: "There is no proven connection between pornography and sexual violence. There have been dozens of reputable studies. Not one has shown any connection." [1] Substitute the words "smoking and lung cancer" in this frequently reiterated defense, of course, and there stands the core argument wielded by the tobacco industry over the decades.

Moreover, the claim that pornography causes harm to at least some users can also be inferred from the fact that some people will go out of their way to avoid encountering pornography, including by paying for software that blocks it. In this way at least some potential consumers signal tacitly their own decision that pornography is potentially injurious— much the same way as the millions who have joined programs to quit smoking, including by paying for them, have also signaled their own consumer view that the substance they want to avoid is injurious too.

There are other intriguing corporate connections as well. Pornography interests today, like tobacco interests, actively enlist the testimony of "experts" who defend their product by arguing a familiar line: that no one has definitively proven that their products can cause "harm". This was, of course,

[1] Nigel Meek, "The Backlash Campaign: Defending S&M Is Defending Individual Freedom", *Individual*, February 2006, p. 10.

exactly the petard on which Big Tobacco was eventually hoisted—but only after many years and many, many millions of dollars went into producing experts disputing the very idea that an ever-higher standard of causal proof had ever been reached.

Similarly, the language of pornography's defense today harmonizes with that of the tobacco industry half a century ago. One hears the same kind of references to constitutional freedom, the same insistence that addiction to the product is a "myth", and the same expressed concern about the necessity of keeping the product away from youth (though the reason why is never explained). In these representative ways, and despite the obvious differences, pornography as an object of dispute in the public square can be argued once more to closely resemble tobacco—not tobacco as we know it today, but tobacco as the object of a hands-off social consensus of, say, fifty years ago.

One more similarity is this. Users of pornography, like users of tobacco, typically develop rationalizations of their habits, or what psychologists call "permission-giving beliefs" that sound identical but for the particular substance in question.

Thus, for example, "everybody does it" is one such belief common to tobacco users yesterday and to pornography consumers today, and common too among those who justify pornography in the public square. "At least I'm not doing something worse" is another such permission-giving rationalization common both to users of nicotine and pornography.

Yet another similar permission-giving belief common to the consumption of both substances is that "this substance [cigarettes, pornography] actually prevents me from doing something worse." In the case of cigarettes, for example, many people justified their use by reference to nicotine's calming effect; and tobacco companies likewise encouraged that defense. As an executive of Philip Morris once remarked,

> What do you think smokers would do if they didn't smoke? You get some pleasure from it, and you also get some other beneficial things, such as stress relief. Nobody knows what you'd turn to if you didn't smoke. Maybe you'd beat your wife. Maybe you'd drive cars fast. Who knows what the hell you'd do?[2]

People today defend pornography along similar lines. Consider the argument arising from time to time that sex crimes in some places have apparently decreased alongside the rise in Internet pornography use. Consider also the resort in both cases to the permission-giving idea that "I'm not affecting anyone but myself."

Moreover, just as pornography and tobacco are both explained by users at the "micro" level with nearly identical rationales, so have both been defended in the public square on nearly identical "macro" grounds: consumer rights. For example, when advocate Wendy McElroy—author of *XXX: A Woman's Right to Pornography*—says, "The issue at stake in the pornography debate is nothing less than the age-old conflict between individual freedom and social control", she is framing the issue of pornography consumption in exactly the way smoking was framed by those who defended it: not as an aesthetic, moral, psychological, or social issue, but as a question of individual right.[3]

---

[2] Quoted in Allan M. Brandt, *The Cigarette Century: The Rise, Fall, and Deadly Persistence of the Product that Defined America* (New York: Basic Books, 2007), p. 430.

[3] Wendy McElroy, *XXX: A Woman's Right to Pornography* (New York: St. Martin's Press, 1997), p. 1.

Finally, it is a fascinating coincidence that both industries have faced similar demographic challenges and opportunities. Most significant, both have had to confront a market imbalance in a crucial demographic—women—and have devised similar strategies for addressing it.

Up until the 1950s, cigarette consumption was far higher among men than among women. The industry's desire to capture the underdeveloped female market led to several imaginative campaigns to increase the level of smoking via new graphics and colors and, above all, via pitches tailored to a female consumer. There followed a series of industry marketing triumphs, among them the breakthrough of Lucky Brand—the first cigarettes targeted for the female audience, in the 1920s—and the later success of Marlboro, which was initially pitched to the female market because its colors matched the red of the then popular nail color. Later campaigns included Phillip Morris' in the 1960s with Virginia Slims, marketed with the slogans "You've come a long way, baby" and "It's a woman thing." Finally, in addition to trying to lure women to "female" brands, the industry also recognized "dual brand" loyalty, or loyalty to brands (like Marlboro) smoked by men as well as women, particularly in the younger demographic.

A similar market gender imbalance faces Internet pornographers today, and the industry is addressing it with much of the same set of strategies. Contemplating the far higher levels of pornography consumption among men, marketers now aggressively target female consumers with gender-tailored bait ranging from softer-core "erotica" focus-tested on women to corporate deals involving new websites, chat rooms, and other media outreach targeting the female demographic.

Most important, and also like tobacco yesterday, Big Porn today further explicitly links its product pitch to the image of the modern, liberated, cool woman. In *The Cigarette*

Century: The Rise, Fall, and Deadly Persistence of the Product that Defined America, a Pulitzer prize–winning history of tobacco mentioned earlier, Allan M. Brandt summarizes the campaigns to create female smokers as follows:

> Smoking for women, in this crucial phase of successful recruitment, became part and parcel of the good life as conceived by the American consumer culture and explicitly represented in advertising campaigns. The effectiveness of these campaigns was heightened and reinforced by public relations efforts to create a positive environment for the new images. Together, the ad campaigns and the PR promoted a product and a behavior that now possessed specific and appealing social meanings of glamour, beauty, autonomy, and equality.[4]

Similar invocations of "autonomy" and "equality" are pitched to today's women as marketers of pornography seek inroads into this demographic. In fact, even before the birth of the Internet, a previous generation of industry entrepreneurs was already trying to break into the female market using "equality" and "liberation" as lures. Thus *Playgirl* magazine, which debuted in 1973 as the first magazine for women showing full frontal male nudity, pitched itself to "today's liberated, independent, self-aware, sensual woman".[5] Similarly, as a pornographic film producer told *Time* magazine in 1987, her movies "stressed equality and the idea that sex was for both women and men, not just men having sex with women".[6]

---

[4] Brandt, *Cigarette Century*, p. 70.

[5] Quoted in Kathleen L. Endres and Therese L. Lueck, *Women's Periodicals in the United States: Consumer Magazines* (West Port, Conn.: Greenwood Publishing Group, 1995), p. 282.

[6] John Leo, "Sexes: Romantic Porn in the Boudoir", *Time*, March 30, 1987, http://www.time.com/time/magazine/article/0,9171,964897,00.html.

In sum, women's liberation has been used in the attempt to sell women on pornography in much the same fashion as it was used to sell women on cigarettes beginning almost a century ago. Feminists often echo this theme themselves in their itinerant defenses of the newer product. No less an authority than Betty Friedan, for example, endorsed the book *Defending Pornography* by ACLU President Nadine Strossen—with the notion that "free expression is an essential foundation for women's liberty, equality and security." [7]

In short, viewing what a stock analyst would call the "fundamentals" of Internet pornography consumption today and comparing them to the "fundamentals" of tobacco consumption yesterday, one finds more similarities than differences between the two. Just as secondhand smoke finally shattered the "so-what?" social consensus about tobacco, so might the potential harms to others ultimately threaten to deep-six the current "so-what?" consensus about pornography.

No doubt some readers find that notion improbable. Yet those who doubt that pornography will ever become the object of restigmatization the way tobacco did overlook a telling social fact: Almost everyone today thinks that the public health campaign against smoking was worth it. This includes many who resented it at the time, and even some people who still smoke. That is the real, and deepest, measure of the victory of the antismoking campaign. Whatever their personal feelings about that campaign yesterday, just about everyone today would agree that tomorrow's generation of kids—at least, of American kids—will be better off

---

[7] Friedan's endorsement appears on the back cover of Nadine Strossen's, *Defending Pornography: Free Speech, Sex, and the Fight for Women's Rights* (New York: NYU Press, 2000), paperback edition.

for not smoking at the same rates that many of their parents and grandparents did.

What seems unremarkable today—accepting pornography industry money for one's charity, say, or serving as judges on Big Porn's award committees, or as "experts" on behalf of its claim that the product does not create addiction or dependency—may seem unreal, and perhaps even noxious, tomorrow. As a corollary, the psychologists and other experts on whom Big Porn depends today may yet live to see their efforts reviled by a future public—just as many people who once aided the tobacco industry, whether paid or not, are seen with our contemporary critical eyes today.

None of this speculation is to say that much will happen overnight to current levels of Internet pornography consumption, or even that such consumption has yet reached its peak. The stigmatization, destigmatization, and restigmatization of behaviors moves slowly compared to the rhythms of any individual, even any given chain of generations. Even so, and despite today's sophisticated consensus about the harmlessness of Internet pornography, it is not hard to imagine a future consensus that casts a colder eye on that substance than does our own—including for reasons that we are only just beginning to understand.

Time itself, it seems safe to wager, will bring a clearer understanding of all aspects of the sexual revolution than we have today; and when it does, pornography will likely be the first stock to be downgraded.

8 The Vindication of *Humanae Vitae*

Of all the paradoxical fallout from the Pill, however, perhaps the most spectacular is this: the most unfashionable,
unwanted, and ubiquitously deplored moral teaching on earth
is also the most thoroughly vindicated by the accumulation
of secular, empirical, postrevolutionary fact. The document
in question is of course *Humanae Vitae*, the encyclical letter
of Pope Paul VI on the subject of the regulation of birth,
published on July 25, 1968.

Now, that *Humanae Vitae* and related Catholic teachings
about sexual morality are laughingstocks in all the best places
is not exactly news. Even in the benighted precincts of believers, where information from the outside world is known to
travel exceedingly slowly, everybody grasps that this is one
doctrine the world loves to hate. During Benedict XVI's
April 2008 visit to the United States, for example, hardly a
story in the secular press failed to mention the teachings of
Humanae Vitae, usually alongside adjectives like "divisive"
and "controversial" and "outdated". In fact, if there's anything on earth that unites the Church's adversaries—all of
them except for the Muslims, anyway—the teaching against
contraception is probably it.

To many people, both today and when the encyclical was
promulgated, the notion simply defies understanding. Consenting adults, told not to use birth control? *Preposterous.*
Third World parents deprived access to contraception and

abortion? *Positively criminal.* A ban on condoms when there's a risk of contracting AIDS? *Beneath contempt.*

"The execration of the world", in philosopher G. E. M. Anscombe's phrase, was what Paul VI incurred with that document—to which the years since 1968 have added plenty of just plain ridicule.[1] Hasn't everyone heard Monty Python's send-up song "Every Sperm Is Sacred"? Or heard the jokes? "You no play-a the game, you no make-a the rules." And "What do you call the rhythm method? *Vatican roulette.*" And "What do you call a woman who uses the rhythm method? *Mommy.*"

As everyone also knows, it's not only the Church's self-declared adversaries who go in for this sort of sport—so, too, do many American and European Catholics, specifically, the ones often called dissenting or cafeteria Catholics, and who more accurately might be dubbed the "Catholic Otherwise Faithful". *I may be Catholic, but I'm not a maniac about it,* runs their unofficial subtext—meaning, *I'm happy to take credit for enlightened Catholic positions on the death penalty, social justice, and civil rights, but, of course, I don't believe in those archaic teachings about divorce, homosexuality, and, above all, birth control.*

Such is the current fate of *Humanae Vitae* and all it represents in the Church in America—and, for that matter, in what is left of the advanced Western one, too. With each passing year, it seems safe to assume, fewer priests can be found to explain the teaching, fewer parishioners to obey it, and fewer educated people to avoid rolling their eyes at the idea that anyone by now could possibly be so antiquarian or purposefully perverse as to hold any opinion about

[1] G. E. M. Anscombe, *Contraception and Chastity* (London: Catholic Truth Society, 1975), reprinted in Janet E. Smith, ed., *Why* Humanae Vitae *Was Right: A Reader* (San Francisco: Ignatius Press, 1993), pp. 121–46.

contraceptive sex—any, that is, other than its full-throttle celebration as the chief liberation of our time.

And in just that apparent consensus about the ridiculousness of it all, amid all those ashes scattered over a Christian teaching stretching back two millennia, arises a fascinating and in fact exceedingly amusing modern morality tale— amusing, at least, to those who take their humor dark.

"He who sits in the heavens laughs" (Ps 2:4), the Psalmist promises, specifically in a passage about enjoying vindication over one's adversaries. If that is so, then the racket by now must be prodigious. Not only have the document's signature predictions been ratified in empirical force, but they have been ratified as few predictions ever are: in ways its authors could not possibly have foreseen, including by information that did not exist when the document was written, by scholars and others with no interest whatever in its teaching, and indeed even inadvertently, and in more ways than one, by many proud public adversaries of the Church.

Forty-plus years after *Humanae Vitae*, fifty-plus after the approval of the Pill, there are more than enough ironies, both secular and religious, to make one swear there's a humorist in heaven.

Let's begin by meditating upon what might be called the first of the secular ironies now evident: *Humanae Vitae*'s specific predictions about what the world would look like if artificial contraception became widespread. The encyclical warned of four resulting trends: a general lowering of moral standards throughout society; a rise in infidelity; a lessening of respect for women by men; and the coercive use of reproductive technologies by governments.

In the years since *Humanae Vitae*'s appearance, numerous distinguished Catholic thinkers have argued, using a variety of evidence, that each of these predictions has been borne out by the social facts. One thinks, for example, of Monsignor George A. Kelly in his 1978 "The Bitter Pill the Catholic Community Swallowed" and of the many contributions of Janet E. Smith, including *Humanae Vitae: A Generation Later* and the edited volume *Why Humanae Vitae Was Right: A Reader.*[2]

And therein lies an irony within an irony. Although it is largely Catholic thinkers who have connected the latest empirical evidence to the defense of *Humanae Vitae*'s predictions, during those same years most of the experts actually *producing* the empirical evidence have been social scientists operating in the secular realm. As sociologist W. Bradford Wilcox emphasized in a 2005 essay, "The leading scholars who have tackled these topics are not Christians, and most of them are not political or social conservatives. They are, rather, honest social scientists willing to follow the data wherever it may lead."[3]

Consider, as Wilcox does, the Nobel Prize–winning economist George Akerlof. In a well-known 1996 article in the *Quarterly Journal of Economics*, Akerlof explained, using the language of modern economics, why the sexual revolution—contrary to common prediction, especially prediction by those

---

[2] Monsignor George A. Kelly, "The Bitter Pill the Catholic Community Swallowed", collected in *The Battle for the Catholic Mind: Catholic Faith and Catholic Intellect in the Work of the Fellowship of Catholic Scholars, 1978–95*, ed. William E. May and Kenneth D. Whitehead (South Bend, Ind.: St. Augustine's Press, 2001, published in association with the Fellowship of Catholic Scholars), pp. 41–109. See also Janet E. Smith, Humanae Vitae: *A Generation Later* (Washington, D.C.: Catholic University of America Press, 1991), and *Why* Humanae Vitae *Was Right* referenced above.

[3] W. Bradford Wilcox, "The Facts of Life and Marriage: Social Science and the Vindication of Christian Moral Teaching", *Touchstone*, January–February, 2005, www.touchstonemag.com/archives/article.php?id=18-01-038-f.

in and out of the Church who wanted the teaching on birth control changed—had led to an increase in both illegitimacy and abortion.[4] In another work published in the *Economic Journal* in 1998, he traced the empirical connections between the decrease in marriage and married fatherhood for men—both clear consequences of the contraceptive revolution—and the simultaneous increase in behaviors to which single men appear more prone: substance abuse, incarceration, and arrests, to name just three.[5]

Along the way, Akerlof found a strong connection between the diminishment of marriage on the one hand and the rise in poverty and social pathology on the other. He explained his findings in nontechnical terms in *Slate* magazine: "Although doubt will always remain about what causes a change in social custom, the technology-shock theory does fit the facts. The new reproductive technology was adopted quickly, and on a massive scale. Marital and fertility patterns changed with similar drama, at about the same time."[6]

To these examples of secular social science confirming what Catholic thinkers had predicted, one might add many more demonstrating the negative effects on children and society. The groundbreaking work that Daniel Patrick Moynihan did in 1965, on the black family, is an example, as is the research of Judith Wallerstein, Barbara Dafoe Whitehead, Sara McLanahan, Gary Sandefur, and David Blankenhorn, among other countercultural scholars mentioned in chapter 1.

---

[4] George A. Akerlof, Janet L. Yellen, and Michael L. Katz, "An Analysis of Out-of-Wedlock Childbearing in the United States", *Quarterly Journal of Economics* 111, no. 2 (1996): 277–317.

[5] George V. Akerlof, "Men Without Children", *Economic Journal* 108 (1998): 287–309.

[6] George V. Akerlof and Janet L. Yellen, "Why Kids Have Kids", November 16, 1996, http://www.slate.com/articles/briefing/articles/1996/11/why_kids_have_kids.html.

Numerous other books followed this path of analyzing the benefits of marriage, including some mentioned earlier in these pages—James Q. Wilson's *The Marriage Problem*, Linda Waite and Maggie Gallagher's *The Case for Marriage*, Kay Hymowitz's *Marriage and Caste in America*, and Elizabeth Marquardt's *Between Two Worlds: The Inner Lives of Children of Divorce*. To this list could be added many more examples of how the data have grown and grown to support the proposition that the sexual revolution has been resulting in disaster for large swaths of the country—a proposition further honed by whole decades of examination of the relation between public welfare and family dysfunction (particularly in the pages of the decidedly not-Catholic *Public Interest* magazine). Still other seminal works have observed that private actions, notably postrevolution sexual habits, were having massive public consequences. Charles Murray's seminal 1984 study of welfare policy, *Losing Ground*, comes especially to mind, as does Francis Fukuyama's influential 1999 book, *The Great Disruption: Human Nature and the Reconstitution of Social Order*.[7]

All this is to say that, beginning just before the appearance of *Humanae Vitae*, an academic and intellectual rethinking began that can no longer be ignored—one whose accumulation of empirical evidence points to the deleterious effects of the sexual revolution on many adults and children. And even in the occasional effort to draw a happy face on current trends, there is no glossing over what are

[7] Charles Murray, *Losing Ground: American Social Policy, 1950–1980* (New York: Basic Books, 1984); Francis Fukuyama, *The Great Disruption: Human Nature and the Reconstitution of Social Order* (New York: Free Press, 1999). Fukuyama called the Pill one of the two most influential features of the age, the other being the shift in labor from a manufacturing to an information-based economy.

still historically high rates of family breakup and unwed motherhood. For example, in a widely discussed and somewhat contrarian essay published in *Commentary* in 2007 called "Crime, Drugs, Welfare—and Other Good News", Peter Wehner and Yuval Levin applauded the fact that various measures of social disaster and dysfunction seem to be improving from previous baselines, including, among others, violent crime and property crime, and teen alcohol and tobacco use. Yet even they had to note that "some of the most vital social indicators of all—those regarding the condition and strength of the American family—have so far refused to turn upward." [8]

In sum, although a few apologists still insist otherwise, just about everyone else in possession of the evidence acknowledges that the sexual revolution has weakened family ties, and that family ties (put simply, the presence of a biologically related mother and father in the home) have turned out to be important indicators of child well-being— and more, that the broken home is not just a problem for individuals but also for society.

Some secular scholars now further link these problems to the contraceptive revolution itself. Consider the work of maverick sociobiologist Lionel Tiger. Hardly a cat's-paw of the pope—he describes religion as "a toxic issue"—Tiger has repeatedly emphasized the centrality of the sexual revolution to today's unique problems. *The Decline of Males*, his 1999 book, was particularly controversial among feminists for its argument that female contraceptives had altered the balance between the sexes in disturbing new ways

---

[8] Yuval Levin and Peter Wehner, "Crimes, Drugs, Welfare—and Other Good News", *Commentary*, December 2007, http://www.commentarymagazine.com/article/crime-drugs-welfare%e2%80%94and-other-good-news/.

(especially by taking from men any say in whether they could have children).[9]

Equally eyebrow-raising, at least in secular circles, is his linking of contraception to the breakdown of families, female impoverishment, trouble in the relationship between the sexes, and single motherhood. Tiger has further argued—as *Humanae Vitae* did not explicitly, though other works of theology have—that "contraception causes abortion".[10]

Who could deny that the predictions of *Humanae Vitae* and, by extension, of Catholic moral theology have been ratified with data and arguments that did not even exist in 1968? But now comes the question that just keeps on giving. Has this dramatic reappraisal of the empirically known universe led to any wider secular reappraisals, however grudging, that Paul VI may have gotten something right after all? The answer is manifestly that it has not. And this is only the beginning of the dissonance that surrounds us.

The years since the Pill's approval have similarly destroyed the mantle called "science" that *Humanae Vitae*'s detractors once wrapped around themselves. In particular, the dooms-day population science so popular and influential during the era in which *Humanae Vitae* appeared has been repeatedly demolished.

Born from Thomas Robert Malthus' famous late-eighteenth-century *Essay on Population*, this was the novel view that humanity itself amounted to a kind of scourge or pollution whose pressure on fellow members would lead to catastrophe. Though rooted in other times and places,

---

[9] Lionel Tiger, *The Decline of Males: The First Look at an Unexpected New World for Men and Women* (Darby, Pa.: Diane Publishing, 1999), p. 20.
[10] Ibid., p. 27.

Malthusianism of one particular variety was fully in bloom in America by the early 1960s. In fact, *Humanae Vitae* appeared two months before the most successful popularization of Malthusian thinking yet: Paul R. Ehrlich's *The Population Bomb*, which opened with the ominous words: "The battle to feed all of humanity is over. In the 1970s and 1980s hundreds of millions of people will starve to death in spite of any crash programs embarked upon now." [11]

If, as George Weigel has suggested, 1968 was absolutely the worst moment for *Humanae Vitae* to appear, it could not have been a better one for Ehrlich to advance his apocalyptic thesis. [12] An entomologist who specialized in butterflies, Ehrlich found an American public, including a generation of Catholics, extraordinarily receptive to his direst thoughts about humanity.

This was the wave that *The Population Bomb* caught on its way to becoming one of the bestsellers of its time. Of course, many people with no metaphysics whatsoever were drawn to Ehrlich's doom-mongering. But for restless Catholics, in particular, the overpopulation scare was attractive— for if overpopulation could be posited as the problem, the putative solution was obvious: *Make* the Church lift the ban on birth control.

[11] Paul Ehrlich, *The Population Bomb: Population Control or Race to Oblivion?* (New York: Sierra Club–Ballantine Books, 1970), p. xi.

[12] See George Weigel, *Witness to Hope: The Biography of Pope John Paul II* (New York: HarperCollins, 1999), p. 210: "The timing of *Humanae Vitae*", he writes, "could not have been worse; 1968, a year of revolutionary enthusiasms, was not the moment for calm, measured reflection on anything. It is doubtful whether any reiteration of the classic Catholic position on marital chastity, no matter how persuasively argued, could have been heard in such circumstances. On the other hand, one has to ask why a position that defended 'natural' means of fertility regulation was deemed impossibly antiquarian at precisely the moment when 'natural' was becoming one of the sacred words in the developed world, especially with regard to ecological consciousness."

It is less than coincidental that the high-mindedness of saving the planet dovetailed perfectly with a more self-interested outcome: the freer pursuit of sexuality via the Pill. Dissenting Catholics had special reasons to stress the "science of overpopulation", and so they did. In the name of a higher morality, their argument went, birth control could be defended as the lesser of two evils (a position argued by the dissenter Charles Curran, among others).

Less than half a century later, these preoccupations with overwhelming birth rates appear practically as pseudoscientific as phrenology. Actually, that may be unfair to phrenology. For the overpopulation literature has not only been abandoned by thinkers for more improved science; it has actually been so thoroughly proved false that today's cutting-edge theory worries about precisely the opposite: a "dearth birth" that is "graying" the advanced world.

In fact, so discredited has the overpopulation science become that by 2008 Columbia University historian Matthew Connelly could publish *Fatal Misconception: The Struggle to Control World Population* and garner a starred review in *Publishers Weekly*—all in service of what is probably the single best demolition of the population arguments that some hoped would undermine Church teaching.[13] This is all the more satisfying a ratification because Connelly is so conscientious in establishing his own personal antagonism toward the Catholic Church (at one point asserting without even a footnote that natural family planning "still fails most couples who try it").

Fatal Misconception is decisive proof that the spectacle of overpopulation, which was used to browbeat the Vatican in the name of science, was a grotesque error all along. First,

---

[13] Matthew Connelly, *Fatal Misconception: The Struggle to Control World Population* (Cambridge, Mass.: Belknap Press, 2008).

Connelly argues, the population-control movement was wrong as a matter of fact: "The two strongest claims population controllers make for their long-term historical contribution" are "that they raised Asia out of poverty and helped keep our planet habitable".[14] Both of these propositions, he demonstrates, are false.

Even more devastating is Connelly's demolition of the claim to moral high ground that the overpopulation alarmists made. For population science was not only failing to help people, Connelly argues, but also actively harming some of them—and in a way that summoned some of the baser episodes of recent historical memory:

> The great tragedy of population control, the fatal misconception, was to think that one could know other people's interests better than they knew it themselves.... The essence of population control, whether it targeted migrants, the "unfit," or families that seemed either too big or too small, was to make rules for other people without having to answer to them. It appealed to people with power because, with the spread of emancipatory movements, it began to appear easier and more profitable to control populations than to control territory. That is why opponents were essentially correct in viewing it as another chapter in the unfinished business of imperialism.[15]

The years since *Humanae Vitae* appeared have also vindicated the encyclical's fear that governments would use the new contraceptive technology coercively. The outstanding example, of course, is the Chinese government's long-running "one-child policy", replete with forced abortions, public trackings of menstrual cycles, family flight, increased

[14] Ibid., p. 371.
[15] Ibid., p. 378.

female infanticide, sterilization, and other assaults too numerous even to begin cataloguing here—in fact, so numerous that they are now widely, if often grudgingly, acknowledged as wrongs even by international human-rights bureaucracies. Lesser-known examples include the Indian government's foray into coercive use of contraception in the "emergency" of 1976 and 1977, and the Indonesian government's practice in the 1970s and 1980s of the bullying implantation of IUDs and Norplant.

Should governments come to "regard this as necessary", *Humanae Vitae* warned, "they may even impose their use on everyone." As with the unintended affirmation by social science, will anyone within the ranks of the population revisionists now give credit where credit is due?

Perhaps the most mocked of *Humanae Vitae*'s predictions was its claim that separating sex from procreation would deform relations between the sexes and "open wide the way for marital infidelity and a general lowering of moral standards". In a day when advertisements for sex scream from every billboard and webpage and when almost every Western family has its share as never before of broken homes and divorce and abortion, some might wonder what further proof could possibly be offered.

But to say that the case is obvious and to leave matters there would be to miss something important. The critical point is, one might say, not so much the proof as the pudding it's in. And it would be hard to get more ironic than having these particular predictions of *Humanae Vitae* vindicated by perhaps the most unlikely—to say nothing of unwilling—witness of all: modern feminism.

Yet that is exactly what has happened since 1968. From Betty Friedan and Gloria Steinem to Andrea Dworkin and

Germaine Greer on up through Susan Faludi and Naomi Wolf, feminist literature has been a remarkably consistent and uninterrupted cacophony of grievance, recrimination, and sexual discontent. In that record—written by the revolution's very *defenders*—we find, as nowhere else, personal testimony of what the revolution has done to womankind. To return to the paradox raised in chapter 2, the liberation of women from the supposed chains of reproduction does not appear to have made womankind happier. In fact, to judge by popular literature, it has made them unhappier than ever—a point that has also been made astutely by a number of contrary-minded social observers including Midge Decter, Danielle Crittenden, and F. Carolyn Graglia.[16]

Consider just what we have been told by endless books on the topic over the years. If feminists married and had children, they lamented it. If they failed to marry or have children, they lamented that, too. If they worked outside the home and also tended their children, they complained about how hard that was. If they worked outside the home and didn't tend their children, they excoriated anyone who thought they should. And running through all this literature is a more or less constant invective about the unreliability and disrespect of men.

The signature metaphors of feminism say everything we need to know about how happy liberation has been making these women: the suburban home as concentration camp,

---

[16] See, among her many other trenchant critiques of feminism, Midge Decter, *An Old Wife's Tale: My Seven Decades in Love and War* (New York: William Morrow, 2001). See also Danielle Crittenden, *What Our Mothers Didn't Tell Us: Why Happiness Eludes the Modern Woman* (New York: Simon and Schuster, 1999), and F. Carolyn Graglia, *Domestic Tranquility: A Brief against Feminism* (Dallas, Tex.: Spence, 1998).

men as rapists, children as intolerable burdens, fetuses as parasites, and so on. These are the sounds of liberation? Even the vaunted right to abortion, both claimed and exercised at extraordinary rates, did not seem to mitigate the misery of millions of these women after the sexual revolution. Coming full circle, feminist and *Vanity Fair* contributor Leslie Bennetts recently published a book urging women to protect themselves financially and otherwise from dependence on men, including from men deserting them later in life. Mothers cannot afford to stay home with their children, she argues, because they cannot trust their men not to leave them. (One of her subjects calls desertion and divorce "the slaughter of the lambs".) Like-minded feminist Linda Hirshman penned a ferocious and widely read manifesto in 2005 urging, among other bitter "solutions", that women protect themselves by adopting—in effect—a voluntary one-child policy.[17] (She argued that a second child often necessitates a move to the suburbs, which puts the office and work-friendly conveniences farther away.)

Beneath all the pathos, the subtext remains the same: Woman's chief adversary is Unreliable Man, who does not understand her sexual and romantic needs and who walks off time and again at the first sashay of a younger thing. What are all these but the generic cries of a woman who thinks that men are "disregarding her physical and emotional equilibrium" and "no longer considering her as his partner whom he should surround with care and affection"?[18]

Perhaps the most compelling case made for traditional marriage lately was not on the cover of, say, *Catholic World Report* but in the devoutly secular *Atlantic*. The 2008 article

[17] Linda Hirshman, "Homeward Bound", *American Prospect*, November 22, 2005.

[18] Pope Paul VI, *Humanae Vitae*, July 25, 1968, 17.

"Marry Him!" by Lori Gottlieb—a single mother who conceived her only child with donor sperm rather than miss
out on motherhood as she has on marriage—is a frank and
excruciatingly personal look into some of the sexual
revolution's lonelier venues, including the creation of children by anonymous or absent sperm donors, the utter cor-
rosiveness of taking a consumerist approach to romance, and
the miserable effects of advancing age on one's sexual
marketability.[19]

Gottlieb writes as one who played by all the feminist
rules, only to realize too late that she'd been had. Beneath
the zippy language, the article runs on an engine of mourn-
ing. Admitting how much she covets the husbands of her
friends, if only for the wistful relief of having someone else
help with the childcare, Gottlieb advises:

> Those of us who choose not to settle in hopes of finding
> a soul mate later are almost like teenagers who believe
> they're invulnerable to dying in a drunk-driving accident.
> We lose sight of our mortality. We forget that we, too,
> will age and become less alluring. And even if some men
> do find us engaging, and they're ready to have a family,
> they'll likely decide to marry someone younger with whom
> they can have their own biological children. Which is all
> the more reason to settle before settling is no longer an
> option.[20]

Like Naomi Wolf and many of the other contemporary
observers mentioned earlier in these pages, Gottlieb is now
just one of many out there giving unwitting testimony to

---

[19] Lori Gottlieb, "Marry Him!", *Atlantic*, February 2008, http://
www.theatlantic.com/magazine/archive/2008/03/marry-him/6651/.
[20] Ibid.

some of the funny things that happened after the Pill freed everybody from sexual slavery once and for all.

That there is no auxiliary literature of grievance for men—who, for the most part, just don't seem to feel they have as much to grieve about in this new world order—is something else that *Humanae Vitae* and a few other retrograde types saw coming in the wake of the revolution. As the saying goes, and as many people did not stop to ask at the time, *cui bono*? Decades later, the evidence is in. As Archbishop Charles J. Chaput observed on *Humanae Vitae*'s thirtieth anniversary in 1998, "Contraception has released males—to a historically unprecedented degree—from responsibility for their sexual aggression." [21] Will any current feminist who honestly disagrees with that statement please stand up?

The adversaries of *Humanae Vitae* also could not have foreseen one important historical development that in retrospect would appear to undermine their demands that the Catholic Church change with the times: the widespread Protestant collapse, particularly the continuing implosion of the Episcopal church and the other branches of Anglicanism. It is about as clear as any historical chain can get that this implosion is a direct consequence of the famous Lambeth Conference in 1930, at which the Anglicans abandoned the longstanding Christian position on contraception. If a church cannot tell its flock "what to do with my body", as the saying goes, with regard to contraception, then other uses of that body will quickly prove to be similarly off-limits to ecclesiastical authority.

[21] Archbishop Charles J. Chaput, 1998 pastoral letter, adapted in "Forty Years Later: Pope's Concern in *Humanae Vitae* Vindicated", *Denver Catholic Register*, July 22, 2008, http://www.archden.org/dcr/news.php?e=480&s=2&a=10086.

It makes perfect if perhaps unfortunate sense, then, that the Anglicans are today imploding over the issue of homosexuality. To quote Anscombe again:

> If contraceptive intercourse is permissible, then what objection could there be after all to mutual masturbation, or copulation in vase indebito, sodomy, buggery (I should perhaps remark that I am using a legal term here—not indulging in bad language), when normal copulation is impossible or inadvisable (or in any case, according to taste)? It can't be the mere pattern of bodily behavior in which the stimulation is procured that makes all the difference! But if such things are all right, it becomes perfectly impossible to see anything wrong with homosexual intercourse, for example. I am not saying: if you think contraception [is] all right you will do these other things; not at all. The habit of respectability persists and old prejudices die hard. But I am saying: you will have no solid reason against these things. You will have no answer to someone who proclaims as many do that they are good too. You cannot point to the known fact that Christianity drew people out of the pagan world, always saying no to these things. Because, if you are defending contraception, you will have rejected Christian tradition.[22]

By giving benediction in 1930 to its married heterosexual members purposely seeking sterile sex, the Anglican church lost, bit by bit, any authority to tell its other members—married or unmarried, homosexual or heterosexual—not to do the same. To put the point another way, once heterosexuals start claiming the right to act as homosexuals, it would not be long before homosexuals started claiming the rights of heterosexuals.

[22] Anscombe, *Contraception and Chastity*, in *Why* HumanaeVitae *Was Right*, p. 136.

Thus in a bizarre but real sense did Lambeth's attempt to show compassion to married heterosexuals inadvertently give rise to the modern gay rights movement—and consequently, to the issues that have divided their church ever since. It is hard to believe that anyone seeking a similar change in Catholic teaching on the subject would want the Catholic Church to follow suit into the moral and theological confusion at the center of today's Anglican church— yet such is the purposeful ignorance of so many who oppose Rome on birth control that they refuse to connect these cautionary historical dots.

The years since *Humanae Vitae* have witnessed something else that neither traditionalist nor dissenting Catholics could have seen coming, one other development shedding retrospective credit on the Church: a serious reappraisal of Christian sexuality from Protestants outside the liberal orbit.

Thus, for instance, Albert Mohler, president of the Southern Baptist Theological Seminary, observed in *First Things* in December 1998, in "Contraception: A Symposium", that "in an ironic turn, American evangelicals are rethinking birth control even as a majority of the nation's Roman Catholics indicate a rejection of their Church's teaching." [23] Later, when interviewed in a 2006 article in the *New York Times* Sunday magazine about current religious thinking on artificial contraception, Mohler elaborated:

> I cannot imagine any development in human history, after the Fall, that has had a greater impact on human beings than the Pill. . . . The entire horizon of the sexual act changes. I think there can be no question that the Pill gave incredible

---

[23] Quoted in R. Albert Mohler Jr., "Can Christians Use Birth Control?", AlbertMohler.com, May 8, 2006 (originally available March 30, 2004), http://www.albertmohler.com/2006/05/08/can-christians-use-birth-control/.

license to everything from adultery and affairs to premarital sex and within marriage to a separation of the sex act and procreation." [24]

Mohler also observed that this legacy of damage was affecting the younger generation of evangelicals. "I detect a huge shift. Students on our campus are intensely concerned. Not a week goes by that I do not get contacted by pastors about the issue. There are active debates going on. It's one of the things that may serve to divide evangelicalism." [25] Part of that division includes Quiverfull, the anticontraception Protestant movement now thought to number in the tens of thousands that further prohibits (as the Catholic Church does not) natural family planning and urges couples to have as many children as they can.

As a corollary to this rethinking by some Protestants, experience seems to have taught a similar lesson to at least some young Catholics—the generation to grow up under divorce, widespread contraception, fatherless households, and all the other emancipatory fallout. As Naomi Schaefer Riley noted in the *Wall Street Journal* about a 2008 contretemps at Notre Dame, "About thirty students walked out of *The Vagina Monologues* in protest after the first scene. And people familiar with the university are not surprised that it was the kids, not the grownups, who registered the strongest objections. The students are probably the most religious part of the Notre Dame [University]. . . . Younger Catholics tend to be among the more conservative ones." [26]

[24] Quoted in Russell Shorto, "Contra-Contraception", *New York Times Magazine*, May 7, 2006, http://www.nytimes.com/2006/05/07/magazine/07contraception.html?pagewanted=all.

[25] Ibid.

[26] Naomi Schaefer Riley, "Rev. John I. Jenkins, Catholicism, Inc.", *Wall Street Journal*, April 12, 2008, http://online.wsj.com/article/SB120796155

Similarly, it is hard to imagine that something like the traditionalist, ecumenical Anscombe Society at Princeton University, started in 2004, could have been founded in 1968 (let alone that a movement dedicated to chastity and traditionalism would also come to have satellites on many other campuses via the Love and Fidelity Network). Nor is there any mistaking that at least some of the return to traditionalism is being spurred by this critical fact, poorly understood in the more sophisticated circles of the West: at least some of the initial victims have come to turn on the revolution itself. As evangelical author Joe Carter has put it, in testimony that many others would echo,

> Having grown up either in a broken home or surrounded by friends who did, we X-Cons [Generation X Conservatives] recognize the value of traditional family structures. We may not always be successful in building permanent relationships ourselves, but we value the bonds of family more than the previous generation.[27]

A similar force making traditionalists of these younger Americans, at least according to some of them, is the fact of their having grown up in a world characterized by abortion on demand. And that brings us to yet another irony worth contemplating on this recent fortieth anniversary: what widespread rejection of *Humanae Vitae* has done to the character of Catholicism in America, specifically.

333509621-search.html?KEYWORDS=Catholicism+Inc+riley&COLLECTION=wsjie/6month.

[27] Joe Carter, "X-Cons: The Conservative Mind of Generation X", *First Things*, from the daily column "On the Square", May 18, 2011, http://www.firstthings.com/onthesquare/2011/05/x-cons-the-conservative-mind-of-generation-x.

As with the other ironies, it helps here to have a soft spot for absurdity. In their simultaneous desire to jettison the distasteful parts of Catholicism and keep the more palatable ones, Catholics in America have done something novel and truly amusing: They have created a specific catalogue of complaints that resembles nothing so much as a Catholic version of the orphan with chutzpah.

Thus many Catholics complain about the dearth of priests, all the while ignoring their own responsibility for that outcome—the fact that few have children in numbers large enough to send one son to the priesthood while the others marry and carry on the family name. They mourn the closing of Catholic churches and schools—never mind that whole parishes, claiming the rights of individual conscience, have contracepted themselves out of existence. They point to the priest sex scandals as proof positive that chastity is too much to ask of people—completely ignoring that it was the randy absence of chastity that created the scandals in the first place.

In fact, the disgrace of contemporary Catholicism—the scandals involving priests and underage boys—is surely traceable at least in part to the collusion between a Catholic laity that wanted a different birth-control doctrine, on the one hand, and a new generation of priests cutting themselves a different kind of slack, on the other. "I won't tattle on my gay priest if you'll give me absolution for contraception" seems to have been the unspoken deal in many parishes since *Humanae Vitae*.

A more obedient laity might have wondered aloud about the fact that a significant number of priests post–Vatican II seemed more or less openly gay. A more obedient clergy might have noticed that plenty of Catholics using artificial contraception were also taking Communion. It is hard to believe that either new development—the widespread open rebellion against Church sexual teachings by the laity, or the concomitant quiet rebellion against Church sexual teachings by a significant number of priests—could have existed without the other.

One has heard a thousand times the insistence that *Humanae Vitae* somehow sparked a rebellion or was something new under the sun. As Peter Steinfels once put the overfamiliar party line, "The pope's 1968 encyclical and the furor it created continue to polarize the American church." [28] On this account, everything was somehow fine until Paul VI refused to bend with the times—at which point all hell broke loose.

To the contrary, all that Paul VI did—as philosopher Anscombe among many other unapologetic Catholics then and since have pointed out—was to reiterate what just about everyone authoritative in the history of Christianity had ever said on the subject until practically the day before yesterday. It was, in a word, no. Just over one hundred years ago, for example, the Lambeth Conference of 1908 affirmed its opposition to artificial contraception in words harsher than anything appearing in *Humanae Vitae*: "demoralizing to character and hostile to national welfare".[29] In another historical

[28] Peter Steinfels, "Vatican Watershed—A Special Report: Papal Birth-Control Letter Retains Its Grip", *New York Times*, August 1, 1993, http://www.nytimes.com/1993/08/01/us/vatican-watershed-a-special-report-papal-birth-control-letter-retains-its-grip.html?pagewanted=all&src=pm.

[29] In addition, three of the 1908 conference's seventy-eight resolutions addressed the subject with a specificity and degree of hostility that would surely come as shocks to most Anglicans today—Resolution 41: "The Conference regards with alarm the growing practice of the artificial restriction of the family, and earnestly calls upon all Christian people to discountenance the use of all artificial means of restriction as demoralising to character and hostile to national welfare." Resolution 42: "The Conference affirms that deliberate tampering with nascent life is repugnant to Christian morality." Resolution 43: "The Conference expresses most cordial appreciation of the services rendered by those medical men who have borne courageous testimony against the injurious practices spoken of, and appeals with confidence

twist that must have someone laughing somewhere, pronouncements of the founding fathers of Protestantism make the Catholic traditionalists of 1968 look positively diffident. Martin Luther in a commentary on the Book of Genesis declared contraception to be worse than incest or adultery. John Calvin called it an "unforgivable crime".[30] The unanimity of Christian teaching on the subject was not abandoned until the year 1930, when the Anglicans voted to allow married couples to use birth control in extreme cases, and one denomination after another over the years came to follow suit.

Seen in the light of actual Christian tradition, the question is not after all why the Catholic Church refused to concede the point; it is rather why just about everyone else in the Judeo-Christian tradition did. Whatever the answer, the Catholic Church took, and continues to take, the public fall for causing a collapse—when actually, in theological and historical terms, she was the only one not collapsing.

From time to time since 1968, some of the Catholics who accepted "the only doctrine that had ever appeared as the teaching of the Church on these things",[31] in Anscombe's words, have puzzled over why, exactly, *Humanae Vitae* has

---

to them and to their medical colleagues to co-operate in creating and maintaining a wholesome public opinion on behalf of the reverent use of the married state" (*The Lambeth Conference: Resolutions Archive from 1908*, published by the Anglican Communion Office, 2005, available online at http://www.lambethconference.org/resolutions/index.cfm).

[30] Quoted in Charles D. Provan, *The Bible and Birth Control* (Monongahela, Pa.: Zimmer Printing, 1989), http://www.jesus-passion.com/contraception.htm.

[31] Janet E. Smith, *Why Humanae Vitae Was Right: A Reader* (San Francisco: Ignatius Press, 1993), p. 132.

been so poorly received by the rest of the world. Surely part of it is timing, as George Weigel observed. Others have cited an implacably secular media and the absence of a national pulpit for Catholics as contributing factors. Still others have floated the idea that John Paul II's *Theology of the Body*, an elaborate and highly positive explication of Christian moral teaching, might have taken some of the sting out of *Humanae Vitae* and better won the obedience of the flock.

At the end of the day, though, it is hard to believe that the fundamental force behind the execration by the world amounts to a phrase here and there in *Humanae Vitae*—or in Augustine, or in Thomas Aquinas, or in the 1930 encyclical *Casti Connubii*, or anywhere else in the long history of Christian teaching on the subject. More likely, the fundamental issue is rather what Archbishop Chaput has explained: "If Paul VI was right about so many of the consequences deriving from contraception, it is because he was right about contraception itself." [32]

This is exactly the connection few people want to make today, because contraceptive sex—as commentators from all over, religious or not, agree—is the fundamental social fact of our time. And the fierce and widespread desire to keep it so is responsible for a great many perverse outcomes. Despite an empirical record that is unmistakably on Paul VI's side by now, there is extraordinary resistance to crediting Catholic moral teaching with having been right about anything, no matter how detailed the record.

Considering the human spectacle today, decades after the document whose widespread rejection reportedly broke

---

[32] Charles J. Chaput, O.F.M. Cap., Archbishop of Denver, "On Human Life: A Pastoral Letter to the People of God of Northern Colorado on the Truth and Meaning of Married Love", July 22, 1998, available online at http://guweb2.gonzaga.edu/~dewolf/chaput.htm.

Paul VI's heart, one can't help but wonder how he and his theologians might have felt if they had glimpsed only a fraction of the evidence now available—whether any of it might have provoked just the smallest wry smile. After all, it would take a heart of stone not to find at least some of what's now out there funny as hell. There is the ongoing empirical vindication in one arena after another of the most unwanted, ignored, and ubiquitously mocked global teaching of the past fifty years. There is the fact that the Pill, which was supposed to erase all consequences of sex once and for all, turned out to have huge consequences of its own. There is the way that so many Catholics, embarrassed by accusations of archaism and driven by their own desires to be as free for sex as everyone around them, went racing for the theological exit signs after *Humanae Vitae*—all this just as the world with its wicked old ways began stockpiling more evidence for the Church's doctrine than anyone living in previous centuries could have imagined, and while still other people were actually being brought closer to the Church because she stood exactly as that "sign of contradiction" when so many in the world wanted otherwise.

Yet instead of vindication for the Church, there is demoralization; instead of clarity, mass confusion; instead of more obedience, ever less. Really, the perversity is, well, perverse. In what other area does humanity operate at this level of extreme, daily, constant contradiction? Where is the Boccaccio for this post-Pill *Decameron*? It really is all very funny, when you stop to think about it. So why isn't everybody down here laughing?

Epilogue

Is the countercultural account offered in this book the whole story of what the sexual revolution has wrought?

Such would be impossible for any single volume, and I do not pretend to have accomplished anything like it here. Moreover, insofar as this book concerns the darker consequences of this vast social movement, it is intrinsically limited in scope. Rather obviously, and as the conventional storyline makes plain, the sexual revolution has made many people happy in this specific and profound sense: It has freed the consumers of modern contraceptives from the natural consequences of their sexual behavior. The pages in this book do not dispute that plain fact. After all, if such unprecedented sexual freedom weren't just what most of the customers ordered, the Pill and its companions would have stayed in their boxes.

Less obviously, though, and as the preceding pages go to show, the specific *sort* of happiness ushered in by the sexual revolution remains a question that for the most part does not get asked today—though it ought to be. To invoke one more analogy between tobacco and sex, one can argue that the sexual revolution has made many people happy in somewhat the way that smoking cigarettes makes smokers happy. Smokers, that is to say, are almost unanimously happy about smoking—until some more or less inevitable crisis brought on by the activity intervenes. Something like *that* kind of happiness, the record presented here may be argued to show, seems also to be true of the fallout from our unprecedented liberations, and unprecedented accompanying problems, in this other realm.

Just about everyone alive today—with the possible exception of those readers who entered a Trappist monastery the second they reached the age of reason and have been living in a cell without windows or the Internet ever since—is implicated one way or another in the sexual revolution. Every family in America by now has been shaped by one or more of its facets—divorce, single parenthood, abortion, cohabitation, widespread pornography, open homosexuality. This fact that we're all in this together also gives people a powerful reason to deny the true costs. After all, who wants to give offense? Who wants one's divorced brother, homosexual cousin, or remarried father to get hurt? The answer is no one, of course—and the desire not to hurt people who are openly living the liberationist creed is yet another reason for the denial we examined in chapter 1.

Yet as the rest of the story presented here has gone to show, there is far more to the legacy of the revolution than is commonly understood. The star athlete with a stable of girls at his sexual command; the young woman whose sexual attractiveness helps with one rung or another of the corporate ladder; the childless CEO with a rich social life who has been catapulted through the glass ceiling because she is unencumbered by family; the well-off childless couple who vacation in the Galapagos and the Himalayas instead of Yellowstone Park or the local campsite—these are indeed some of the faces of the sexual revolution's children, and as snapshots they look happy indeed.

There are other faces too, though, and they have stories of their own—stories that as the foregoing chapters go to show are increasingly well-documented, whether wittingly or not, by social scientists and other secular authorities. They include the young women on campus and elsewhere exploited by men whose expectations have been warped by the revolution's false promises; the older women who bought the revolution's rhetoric of sexual equality, only to find too late that marriage and motherhood won't be for them; the men caught in one or another back room at the revolution's wild party who discovered, also too late, that they couldn't get back home again after all. And there remain the children who have faced, and continue to face, all manner of higher risks in their lives because the sexual revolution helped to disrupt their lives or to empower adults with sinister designs on them.

These other people—these unseen victims of what may yet, per Sorokin, turn out to be the grandest and least understood human experiment of our time—are also part of any reckoning of what the revolution has wrought, or ought to be. They and others like them are the human reasons for this book. It is my hope that the evidence presented herein may make a modest contribution toward bringing this other part of the revolution's legacy to light—and with it, a clearer understanding of modern man and woman than exists in the current, often willful, misunderstanding of what that revolution has really wrought.

Index